The POWER
of PRAYING
in TONGUES

The POWER
of PRAYING
in TONGUES

**unleashing
the supernatural
dimension in you**

Glenn Arekion

DESTINY IMAGE™ EUROPE srl
Via Maiella, 1
66020 San Giovanni Teatino (Ch) – Italy

"Changing the world, one book at a time."

This book and all other Destiny Image™ Europe books are available at Christian bookstores and distributors worldwide.

To order products, or for any other correspondence:

DESTINY IMAGE™ EUROPE srl
Via Acquacorrente, 6
65123 - Pescara - Italy
Tel. +39 085 4716623 - Fax: +39 085 9431270
E-mail: info@eurodestinyimage.com
Or reach us on the Internet: www.eurodestinyimage.com

ISBN: 978-88-96727-09-6
For Worldwide Distribution, Printed in the U.S.A.
1 2 3 4 5 6 7 8/13 12 11 10

I thank my God that I speak in tongues more than ye all
(1 Corinthians 14:18).

DEDICATION

To my Lord and Savior Jesus Christ, You are my God and my Majesty. I bow my knee to you.

To my wife, Rosanna, the greatest gift that God ever gave to me and my three amazing children, thank you for making my life easy. Lisa, you are my pride; Ethan, you are the greatest son in the world; Jodie, you bring joy to my life.

To my parents, Clency and Marlene Arekion, without your love, discipline, and guidance where would I be and who would I be? Thank you.

To my two brothers, Bruno and James Arekion, you guys are my pillars! I do not have enough words to describe your importance to me.

To Pastor Tom and Barbara Jeffery...simply the greatest people in the world.

TABLE OF CONTENTS

INTRODUCTION

But, beloved, remember ye the words which were spoken before of the apostles of our Lord Jesus Christ; how that they told you there should be mockers in the last time, who should walk after their own ungodly lusts. These be they who separate themselves, sensual, having not the Spirit. But ye, beloved, building up yourselves on your most holy faith, praying in the Holy Ghost (Jude 1:17-20).

One of the greatest ministers who ever graced this earth was Reverend John G. Lake. Although he went through terrible hardships, he was a world shaker. What was the secret to John G. Lake's deep revelations, extraordinary manifestations, and the success of his ministry? Here is an excerpt from his own mouth: "I want to talk with the utmost frankness and say to you, *that tongues have been the making of my ministry.* It is that peculiar communication with God when God reveals to my soul the truth I utter to you day by day in the ministry....Many times, I climb out of bed, take my pencil and pad, and jot down the beautiful things of God, the wonderful things of God that He talks out in my spirit and reveals to my heart."[1]

Notice these words: "Tongues have been the making of my ministry." Tongues will be the making of your life. As you read and look through this book, you will find the missing element in your life. Give yourself to prayer! Develop your relationship with the Holy Spirit and become sensitive to His leadings as you sharpen your receptivity to His voice through tongues. As revealed in the tiny Book of Jude, it is one of the greatest keys for effective living in the last days. While everything in the world is heading south, your life will head in the direction of success through the Holy Spirit.

Another great man who knew the power of *praying in tongues* was Smith Wigglesworth. Here was an uneducated plumber who, when he partook of the blessing of *tongues*, was transformed into the *apostle of faith*. The miracles, boldness, and manifestation of the supernatural became evident in his life and ministry. This is what the world is looking for! John the Baptist said, "I indeed baptize you with water unto repentance: but He that cometh after me is mightier than I, whose shoes I am not worthy to bear: He shall baptize you with the Holy Ghost, and with fire"(Matt. 3:11). Get ready to be on fire for God and with God. Get ready for an adventure of a lifetime!

ENDNOTE

1. http://www.tentmaker.org/holy-spirit/baptism1.htm; accessed April 06, 2010.

Chapter 1

THE IMPORTANCE
OF PRAYER

Now about that time Herod the king stretched forth his hands to vex certain of the church. And he killed James the brother of John with the sword. And because he saw it pleased the Jews, he proceeded further to take Peter also....Peter therefore was kept in prison: but prayer was made without ceasing of the church unto God for him (Acts 12:1-3,5).

And he spake a parable unto them to this end, that men ought always to pray, and not to faint (Luke 18:1).

Be earnest and unwearied and steadfast in your prayer [life], being [both] alert and intent in [your praying] with thanksgiving (Colossians 4:2 AMP).

Prayer is a command and calling of God. The Lord Jesus Christ specifically mentioned that His house is to be the house of prayer: "And said unto them, It is written, My house shall be called the house of prayer..." (Matt. 21:13). The word *house* in Greek is the word *oikos*, and it also means "family."[1] In essence, the Lord was stating that His family was to be a family of prayer. If you are born again, then you form part of the family of God, and prayer is your calling. First and foremost, prayer is communion with God. It is the

13

spirit of humanity communing and fellowshipping with God, who is the Father of all spirits.

Essentially, prayer is spirit to Spirit communion, and there is tremendous power in it. Many believers know this fact in their head, but they do not know it as a living experience in their lives. When evil King Herod raised an attack against the very existence of the early Church, the believers saw "unceasing prayer" as the sole response to the attacks of satan. Prayer was a major pillar in the early Church. That's why we see the devotions of the Church to this pillar. The apostle Paul declared in his Roman epistle, "continuing instant in prayer" (Rom. 12:12).

Unfortunately, many believers do not know the reality of this verse, and that is why there is little manifestation of power in their lives. It is not the will of God for you to walk in little power when all of His ability is available to you. There is no doubt about it, a failure of power is a failure of prayer. Failure to pray is failure in all of life. Today, I want you to realize that people who do not pray are robbing themselves of the help of the Almighty. The early Church knew and understood the priority and potency of prayer. Look at this horrific situation that took place in the twelfth chapter of Acts:

> *Now about that time **Herod the king stretched forth his hands to vex** certain of **the church**. And he killed James the brother of John with the sword. And because he saw it pleased the Jews, he proceeded further to take Peter also. (Then were the days of unleavened bread.) And when he had apprehended him, he put him in prison, and delivered him to four quaternions of soldiers to keep him; intending after Easter to bring him forth to the people. Peter therefore was kept in prison: but prayer was made without ceasing of the church unto God for him* (Acts 12:1-5).

The word *vex* means "to hurt and harm." According to the apostle Paul, we wrestle not against flesh and blood, but against principalities, powers, and wicked spirits (see Eph. 6:12). In Acts 12, satan was behind the scene; he was the puppet master, and Herod was the puppet on a string. This act of violence was more than just Herod doing a popular thing against believers and more than just a haphazard attack of the enemy. This was a calculated and pre-meditated act of satan to destroy the Church. Notice that three specific names are mentioned in this event—Peter, James, and John. There is nothing in the Word by accident! Every word and name has a purpose and meaning. Why are their names mentioned? Of what significance is it that these three names are mentioned?

> *And when James, Cephas, and John, who seemed to be pillars...* (Galatians 2:9).

This was Paul's testimony of the three mentioned names. Paul saw them as pillars in the church, and pillars hold up the building. If you remove the pillars, then the building collapses. This is an even clearer picture of the attack that came against the early Church.

PLAN, PURPOSE, AND PROCEDURE

In killing James, Herod removed one pillar; and in going after Peter, he was endeavoring to remove another pillar. Satan was after the destruction of the Church. He had a devious plan with the purpose of destroying the very existence of the Church and had a procedure to get it done. Now, we know the James who is mentioned in Paul's letter to the Galatians was the brother of our Lord, and the one beheaded was the brother of John. Nonetheless, we could agree that the son of Zebedee was also a pillar—as his brother John before his decapitation. *Remove the pillars and I can destroy the church, satan thought.* However, look at the way the early Church responded to an onslaught against them:

> *Peter therefore was kept in prison: but prayer was made without ceasing of the church unto God for him* (Acts 12:5).

INTERVENTION

Through unceasing prayer, the church stopped the assignment of the devil and his onslaught of attacks. Prayer raised the wall of defense against future attacks of satan. Prayer means "to make an intervention."

To pray means to intervene. What does it mean to intervene?

Intervention is...

- To come in between so as to prevent or alter a result or course of events.[2]
- Act of stepping in the middle to stop an oncoming attack.

Prayer is divine intervention.

My Younger Brother Bruno

I have two younger brothers—Bruno and James. Today, all three of us are in the ministry and all three of us are pastors. However, there was a time when we were heathens, and then there was a time when we got saved but were still carnal believers. With three boys in the house, there were some major fights while we were growing up. James is five years younger than I, so he was easy to handle and slap around when we were kids, but Bruno was a little more complicated and a little more than I could handle. He is only one year younger and bigger than I am. With a name like *Bruno*, I had problems on my hands.

I will never forget the time during our teen years when Bruno bought new Puma sneakers with money he earned at his part-time job. I did not have a job, but I wanted new sneakers—*his* new sneakers. He had hidden them under his bed, but on a Saturday while he was at work, I decided to take his new Puma sneakers and go out, thinking that I would put them back under the bed before he returned home. Well! That didn't go quite as I planned, as he got home before I did. When I walked into the kitchen, there he was. Now, there is one interesting fact to note about my brother. When he was younger, when he got angry or tired, one of his eyes went cockeyed. As I opened the kitchen door, Bruno stood and his eye caught what I was wearing.

I am so busted, I thought. His one cockeye was working overtime, zooming left and right like the red light on Kitt the Knight Rider car. He started to interrogate me, and before I could answer he punched me. Having quick reflex, I swerved. Nonetheless, he caught my left ear, and as I swerved, my right ear hit the kitchen door that was ajar. I ducked down and held both ears as I didn't know which ear to hold. They both hurt at the same time. Then I felt heat pass by my face. I was angry.

I thought to myself, *Today one of us is going to die; this kitchen is not big enough for us.* I mustered all my strength and focused it in my left fist, as I am left handed. I was thinking to myself, *I'm going to lay hands on you and you will not recover!* I was ready to launch my attack, and just when I was about to make contact with my brother's eye, my mother intervened. She stepped in the middle of us two. As quickly as my fist was heading toward his face, I pulled back. I knew if I had hit my mother, then my father would have killed me. My mother stepped in the middle to stop an oncoming attack. She stepped in the middle to alter the course of events.

That is intervention. That is what happens when you pray. Satan may be advancing against you ready to knock you out, but if you pray, God will step in the middle, stop the attack, and alter the course of events. Are you willing to pay the price to pray? Are you willing to raise the pillar of prayer? Are you willing to stop the attacks of the devil? Pray and God will intervene.

> *And, behold, the angel of the Lord came upon him, and a light shined in the prison: and he smote Peter on the side, and raised him up, saying, Arise up quickly. And his chains fell off from his hands* (Acts 12:7).

Every chain of the enemy will be broken as you pray. God is no respecter of persons (see Acts 10:34). If He did it for Peter and the early Church, He will do it for you. Supernatural breakthroughs were a reality to the early believers because their lives were saturated with prayer. As a believer or minister who desires the supernatural edge in your life, it is imperative that you develop a strong prayer life or strong prayer base. The life of prayer and increase in the anointing go hand in hand. There is a direct connection between prayer and power. If you are to grow in the anointing, it is of utmost importance that you develop a strong prayer life. This is where the modern Church or believer is missing it. Without prayer, the Church will be just a social gathering without the presence and the power of God. If you want revival you need to pray; if you want to see signs and wonders, you need to pray; if you want lives to be changed by mighty healings and deliverances, you need to pray.

You might say, "Well, I've been praying!" What is the evidence that you have been praying? The Bible says, "...the earnest (heartfelt, continued) prayer of a righteous man makes tremendous power available [dynamic in its working]" (James 5:16 AMP). Power is the token that you have been praying. If you do not see any manifestation of power in your life, then something needs to change. "For I am the Lord, I do not change..." (Mal. 3:6 AMP).

Since God does not change, you need to. Many have changed theology to fit their lack of power or shortcomings. The excuses are many, but the reason is simply that lack of prayer equals lack of power.

Second Chronicles 7:14 says, "If My people, which are called by My name, shall humble themselves, and pray, and seek, [crave, and require of necessity] My face and turn from their wicked ways; then will I hear from heaven, and will forgive their sin, and will heal their land."

The choice is yours. If you are praying already, pray more. When William Seymour met with John G. Lake in a Chicago hotel room prior to the Azusa outpouring, he told him he had been praying for five hours a day. Seymour told John G. Lake what the Spirit told him when he asked, "What else must I do to experience revival?" The Holy Spirit replied, "Pray more!" God had led this man into a deep life of prayer, assigning five hours every day for prayer. This prayer life continued for over three years. As he was praying one day, the Holy Ghost said to him, "There are better things to be had in the spiritual life, but they must be sought out with faith and prayer." After this instruction, William Seymour increased his hours of prayer to seven hours and continued to pray in the same vein for two years. And the rest is history. John Wesley also said, "It seems God doesn't do anything unless we pray."

> *But we will give ourselves continually to prayer, and to the ministry of the word* (Acts 6:4).

The excuses for lacking spiritual growth are many, but the reason is simply that lack of prayer equals lack of power.

The foundational apostles knew the secret to success was in total devotion to prayer. They knew that they could not neglect prayer. Even when they became very busy in ministry, they did not allow business to get in the way of prayer. Even when the church was growing at a rapid rate in the sixth chapter of Acts, the apostles did not neglect the service and necessity of prayer:

> *And in those days, when the number of the disciples was multiplied, there arose a murmuring of the Grecians against the Hebrews, because their widows were neglected in the daily ministration. Then the twelve called the multitude of the disciples unto them, and said, It is not reason that we should leave the word of God, and serve tables. Wherefore, brethren, look ye out among you seven men of honest report, full of the Holy Ghost and wisdom, whom we may appoint over this business. But we will give ourselves continually to prayer, and to the ministry of the word* (Acts 6:1-4).

I specially love the way the New International Version translates this particular verse, *"and will give our attention to prayer and the ministry of the word."* The early Church gave great attention to and was highly dedicated to the subject of prayer. Today satan has, to a certain degree, removed prayer from the Church. While it is disturbing that prayer has been removed from public schools in the United States of America and the nations of the world, it is even more disturbing to realize that for the most part prayer has been removed from the Church.

Prayerlessness is rampant in most churches, and that is why we have lost our effectiveness. Pastors from all around the world will tell you that prayer meeting is the least attended service. Many church leaderships rely on gimmicks and guest ministers to bring revival to their churches. Revival may come through some ministers, but when they leave, the revival may also leave. What we spend a lot of money to obtain can be accessed freely in prayer. God's instruction to His Church is still, "Pray without ceasing" (1 Thess. 5:17). The words of Jesus are still for us today, "Men ought always to pray, and not to faint" (Luke 18:1). "Be earnest and unwearied and steadfast in your prayer [life], being [both] alert and intent in [your praying] with thanksgiving" (Col. 4:2 AMP).

ENDNOTES

1. Strong's Concordance #G3624, s.v. *house*.
2. New Oxford American Dictionary Oxford University Press, USA; 2 edition (May 19, 2005) s.v. *intervention*.

Chapter 2

PRAYING IN THE SPIRIT

Pray without ceasing (1 Thessalonians 5:17).

The apostle Paul, coming to the end of his epistle to the Thessalonians, instructed them to pray without stopping. The Living Bible puts it clearly, "Always keep on praying." Prayer is an important aspect of Church life, and we are told to pray constantly. How then do we pray without ceasing?

> *Praying always with all prayer and supplication in the Spirit, and watching thereunto with all perseverance and supplication for all saints* (Ephesians 6:18).

> *Pray at all times (on every occasion, in every season) in the Spirit...* (Ephesians 6:18 AMP).

> *And pray in the Spirit on all occasions with all kinds of prayers and requests...* (Ephesians 6:18 NIV).

> *Pray in the Spirit at all times and on every occasion...* (Ephesians 6:18 NLT).

> *Use every kind of prayer and entreaty, and at every opportunity pray in the spirit...* (Ephesians 6:18 Goodspeed Version).

Paul gives us a powerful key as to how we can keep on praying without letting up. He said to pray always in the spirit. What is praying in the spirit? The term *praying in the spirit* is mentioned several times in the Scriptures.

> *For he that speaketh in an unknown tongue speaketh not unto men, but unto God: for no man understandeth him; howbeit in the spirit he speaketh mysteries* (1 Corinthians 14:2).

> *So what shall I do? I will pray with my spirit, but I will also pray with my mind; I will sing with my spirit, but I will also sing with my mind* (1 Corinthians 14:15 NIV).

HEAVENLY PRAYER LANGUAGE

So, what exactly does it mean to pray in the spirit? There are those who do not believe in "glossolalia"—that is "speaking with other tongues," and they disdain this phenomenon. They say that praying in the spirit is prayer that is led and guided by the Holy Spirit. Well, of course, we certainly believe that! All prayer should be led by the Holy Spirit and out of your spirit. However there are two kinds of Spirit-led prayer. One is done with the mind engaged in your known tongue and the other with the mind bypassed. Paul advocates this when he said, "I will pray with the spirit, but I will also pray with the understanding" (1 Cor. 14:15).

Praying *with* the spirit is synonymous to praying *in* the spirit and synonymous to "...as the Spirit gave them utterance" as recorded in Acts 2:4. What happened when the Spirit enabled or gave them utterance? They spoke in other tongues. What is called Spirit-led prayers and "praying in the spirit" is to pray in tongues as Paul aptly describes to the Corinthian saints, "For he that speaketh in an unknown tongue speaketh not unto men, but unto God...howbeit *in the spirit* he speaketh mysteries (1 Cor. 14:2).

Praying in the spirit is praying in your heavenly prayer language of tongues. Some have said, "Tongues is of the devil!" However, the Book of Acts states that tongues are "the wonderful works of God" (see Acts 2:11). If praying in tongues was evil, then Paul would have been demon possessed because he said, "I thank my God, I speak with tongues more than ye all" (1 Cor. 14:18). Isn't that uncanny and preposterous for people to come up with such an excuse?

Other excuses that we hear today are, "Speaking in tongues is not for us today." Then why would the apostle Paul waste his time talking about tongues in the function of a church service in the fourteenth chapter of the Book of Corinthians? The apostle Paul also said, "Forbid not to speak with tongues" (1 Cor. 14:39), and then he uttered these powerful words, "I would that ye all spake with tongues…" (1 Cor. 14:5). You cannot pick and choose what part of Paul's writings are from God and what parts are his own ideas. The apostle Paul did state these words, "But to the rest speak I, not the Lord…" (1 Cor. 7:12), but I believe that he was not referencing tongues. Praying and speaking in tongues are a fulfillment of the prophecy Jesus announced on the day of His ascension.

Paul is speaking the mind of God on the matter of tongues; therefore, we must hear what he has to say and live in the light of it. Speaking and praying in other tongues is for us today. The issue in the early Church, unlike the modern Church, was not whether people spoke in tongues or not, but rather how much they spoke in tongues. The apostle Paul said, "I thank my God, I speak with tongues more than you all" (see 1 Cor. 14:18). That was the secret to his supernatural life, revelations, and ministry. The Lord General of the Church, Jesus Christ Himself declared that the believer would speak in tongues:

> *And these signs shall follow them that believe; In My name shall they cast out devils; they shall speak with new tongues* (Mark 16:17).

When you are praying in tongues, you are in good company, and you are not out of order. It does not matter what some denominations say or argue. If the Lord has said that the believer will speak with new tongues, then the matter is settled. You are right in the plan of God when you pray in tongues. On the day of Pentecost when the Spirit of God made His grand entry as promised by the Father, the Word records:

*And they were all filled with the Holy Ghost, and began
to speak with other tongues as the Spirit gave them utterance* (Acts 2:4).

Do you think the Holy Spirit will give something detrimental to
your spiritual welfare? No! Jesus said He will guide you into all the
truth, as He is the Spirit of truth (see John 16:13). The devil will do
his best to keep you away from tongues because he knows that if
you tap into this power then you will no longer be a victim of circumstances. He has come up with all kinds of lies to discount the
marvelous prayer language.

*And He said unto them, Go ye into all the world, and
preach the gospel to every creature. And these signs shall
follow them that believe; In My name shall they cast out
devils; they shall speak with new tongues* (Mark 16:15,17).

In a later chapter, we will look more acutely at other "so-called"
defenses against glossolalia, but another excuse that has been propagated by theologians who are "anti-tongues" is that *new tongues*
meant that there won't be any cussing in your mouth. It is true there
should not be profanity in the mouth of the believer, but this is not a
new thing. Other theologians have said that *tongues* is an ability
given to preach the Gospel in the language of foreigners, citing the
second chapter of Acts. If that was the case then the tongues that
Peter and the disciples spoke would be old languages that already
existed. This theory does not hold water, as none of those who
heard the disciples speaking in other tongues was saved until Peter
spoke or preached in his own tongue. On the day of Pentecost Peter
did not preach in tongues, but he preached in his own tongue and
three thousand souls were added to the Church.

*And they were all filled with the Holy Ghost, and began to
speak with other tongues, as the Spirit gave them utterance. And there were dwelling at Jerusalem Jews, devout
men, out of every nation under heaven. Now when this
was noised abroad, the multitude came together, and were
confounded, because that every man heard them speak in
his own language.And they were all amazed and mar-
velled, saying one to another, Behold, are not all these*

which speak Galilaeans? And how hear we every man in our own tongue, wherein we were born? (Acts 2:4-8)

And these signs shall follow them that believe; In My name shall they cast out devils; they shall speak with new tongues (Mark 16:17).

TONGUES FOR US TODAY

In the Great Commission as stated in the last chapters of the Gospels of Matthew and Mark (see Matt. 28:19-20; Mark 16:15-18), Jesus said that a sign that will follow the New Testament believer is speaking in new tongues. The word *new* is the same Greek word that is used when Paul used the term new creature.

Therefore if any man be in Christ, he is a new creature: old things are passed away; behold, all things are become new (2 Corinthians 5:17).

The Greek word for "new" is *kainos* and it means:

- Something new and unheard of
- Of a new kind
- A brand-new species that never existed before
- Fresh and new[1]

When you became a born-again believer, you became a brand-new species of being that never existed before. Likewise, speaking in tongues is a brand-new thing that never existed before. It is something recently made, of a new kind, unprecedented, novel, uncommon, unheard of. It was not so in the time of Abraham, Moses, Elijah, and John the Baptist, but it certainly is so after the resurrection. Paul spoke in tongues, as did the apostles Peter and John and the 120 believers in the upper room on the day of Pentecost. That is why we do not see tongues mentioned in the Old Testament. Speaking or praying in tongues was and is a new phenomenon that belongs to believers on this side of the cross and resurrection. New tongues should be spoken by those of the new birth.

As a believer or minister who endeavors to increase in the anointing, you have to develop the art of praying in the Spirit. "Now concerning spiritual *gifts* brethren, I would not have you ignorant" (1 Cor. 12:1).

> ## New tongues should be spoken by those of the new birth.

THE SUPERNATURAL

In the King James Version of First Corinthians 12:1, the word *gifts* is italicized. This means it was put there at the discretion of the translators supposedly to help us. Whenever you see a word italicized in the Authorized Version, it simply means that the particular word is not in the original text. This verse should literally be read as "Now concerning spiritual, brethren, I would not have you ignorant." The twelfth chapter of Corinthians does not just deal with the gifts of the Spirit but also with ministries and the Body of Christ. The word *spiritual* is the Greek word *pneumatikos* and it means:[2]

- Things pertaining to the Spirit
- Supernatural
- The Miraculous
- Movement of the wind of God

So this verse can be rendered as follows:

- Now concerning things pertaining to the Spirit, brothers, I would not have you ignorant.
- Now concerning the supernatural, brothers, I do not want you ignorant.
- Now concerning the miraculous, brothers, I do not want you ignorant.
- Now concerning the movement of the wind of God, brothers, I do not want you ignorant.

The supernatural and the realm of the miraculous are for the believer. Witchcraft, psychics, tarot card readers, fortune telling, druids, wizards, witches, warlocks, and New Agers are not the inventors of and do not monopolize the supernatural. What the occult calls *supernatural* is demonic infestation. The supernatural and the miraculous are for the believer. The twelfth to the fourteenth chapters of Corinthians speak of several supernatural topics such as:

- Gifts of the Spirit
- Ministries
- Body of Christ, the Church
- Love
- Diversities of Tongues
- Tongues as a prayer language
- Prophecy
- Tongues and prophecy in church service

What the occult calls "supernatural" is demonic infestation.

In First Corinthians 12:10, Paul declares, "...to another divers kinds of tongues...." The Weymouth rendering of this verse is, "... to another varieties of the gift of tongues, to another the interpretation of tongues." Basically, there are four major varieties or kinds of tongues in the New Testament:

- Tongues for personal edification—personal heavenly prayer language
- Tongues for interpretation—an utterance or message in tongues
- Tongues for intercession—groanings and standing in the gap
- Tongues as a sign to unbelievers

Growing and increasing in the anointing will require that you spend much time praying in tongues or praying in the spirit. As already mentioned, we realize that "praying in the spirit" can also be defined as

27

prayer that is led by the Holy Spirit in your known language, but as a rule praying in the spirit is synonymous to praying in tongues.

In the next chapter I discuss many benefits of praying in tongues. Like Paul, I thank God I can speak in tongues on a daily and regular basis, thus partaking of the great multifaceted benefits it renders. Remember, satan and well-meaning but ignorant people will do their utmost to keep you away from tongues, but you must press in to this glorious gift. Allow me to give you a working definition of tongues as a prayer language. Tongues is supernatural utterance by the Holy Spirit in a language never learned by the person doing the speaking or praying. Tongues is the language of the supernatural realm just like French is the language of France. If you want to be effective and be understood in France, then you should know how to speak French because that is what they speak in that part of the world. If we want to be effective in the supernatural realm, then we have to become acquainted with the supernatural language of tongues.

Now let's delve into the manifold benefits of tongues as a private supernatural prayer language.

ENDNOTES

1. Strong's Concordance #G2537, s.v. *new*.
2. W.E. Vine, *Vines Expository of Greek New Testament Words* #3466 (Nashville, TN: Thomas Nelson).

Chapter 3

THE DEBACLE OF CESSATIONISM DOCTRINE

And they were all filled with the Holy Ghost, and began to speak with other tongues, as the Spirit gave them utterance (Acts 2:4).

I'd like to make this point very clear: you do not need the baptism of the Holy Spirit with the evidence of speaking in other tongues to be saved. Second, if you are saved, then you already have the Holy Spirit. It is erroneous to say if a person does not speak or pray in tongues that the latter does not have the Holy Spirit. Tongues has nothing to do with your salvation or you having the Holy Spirit. When a person receives salvation, then this person becomes the temple of the Holy Spirit. As a born-again child of God, the Holy Spirit is already inside of you. He is in your life already. The baptism of the Holy Spirit with tongues is another blessing altogether. These are two different things.

Even though every believer who has received Christ is definitely saved and has the indwelling Holy Spirit, not every believer has been baptized in the Holy Spirit. He or she has been baptized into Christ and has been born of the Spirit. Salvation and the baptism in the Holy Spirit are two separate and contrasting experiences. They are different as to time and nature. As already mentioned and now re-emphasized, a person can receive salvation without experiencing the baptism of the Holy Spirit. A believer does not need the baptism of the Holy Spirit with tongues to be saved. A person is saved by confessing the Lordship of Christ Jesus with his mouth and believing in his heart, as Paul stated to the Romans saints, "That if thou shalt confess with thy mouth the Lord Jesus, and shalt believe in thine heart that God hath raised him from the dead, thou shalt be saved" (Rom. 10:9).

To reiterate, you do not need tongues in order to be saved but you cannot receive the baptism of the Holy Spirit without first experiencing salvation. Therefore, the baptism of the Holy Ghost with the evidence of speaking in other tongues must be preceded by salvation, the recreation, and regeneration of your spirit. We can see this evidenced in Luke's systematic treatise to Theophilus, where he listed five events:

- The 120 disciples in the Upper Room in Jerusalem

  And when the day of Pentecost was fully come, they were all with one accord in one place. And suddenly there came a sound from heaven as of a rushing mighty wind, and it filled all the house where they were sitting. And there appeared unto them cloven tongues like as of fire, and it sat upon each of them. And they were all filled with the Holy Ghost, and began to speak with other tongues, as the Spirit gave them utterance (Acts 2:1-4).

- The Samaritan believers

  Now when the apostles which were at Jerusalem heard that Samaria had received the word of God, they sent unto them Peter and John: Who, when they were come down, prayed for them, that they might receive the Holy Ghost: (For as yet he was fallen upon none of them: only they were baptized in the name of the Lord Jesus.) Then laid they their hands on them, and they received the Holy Ghost. And when Simon saw that through laying on of the apostles' hands the Holy Ghost was given, he offered them money, Saying, Give me also this power, that on whomsoever I lay hands, he may receive the Holy Ghost (Acts 8:14-19).

- The apostle Paul

And as he journeyed, he came near Damascus: and suddenly there shined round about him a light from heaven: And he fell to the earth, and heard a voice saying unto him, Saul, Saul, why persecutest thou me? **And he said, Who art thou, Lord?** *And the Lord said, I am Jesus whom thou persecutest: it is hard for thee to kick against the pricks. And he trembling and astonished said, Lord, what wilt thou have me to do? And the Lord said unto him, Arise, and go into the city, and it shall be told thee what thou must do...And Ananias went his way, and entered into the house; and putting his hands on him said,* **Brother Saul, the Lord, even Jesus, that appeared unto thee in the way as thou camest, hath sent me, that thou mightest receive thy sight, and be filled with the Holy Ghost.** *And immediately there fell from his eyes as it had been scales: and he received sight forthwith, and arose, and was baptized* (Acts 9:3-6,17-18).

- The household of Cornelius

While Peter yet spake these words, the Holy Ghost fell on all them which heard the word. And they of the circumcision which believed were astonished, as many as came with Peter, because that on the Gentiles also was poured out the gift of the Holy Ghost. For they heard them speak with tongues, and magnify God... (Acts 10:44-46).

- The Ephesian believers

And it came to pass, that, while Apollos was at Corinth, Paul having passed through the upper coasts came to Ephesus: and finding certain disciples, He said unto them, Have ye received the Holy Ghost since ye believed? And they said unto him, We have not so much as heard whether there be any Holy Ghost. And he said unto them, Unto what then were ye baptized? And they said, Unto John's baptism. Then said Paul, John verily baptized with the baptism of repentance, saying unto the people, that they should believe on Him which should come after him, that is, on Christ Jesus. When they heard this, they were baptized in the name of the Lord Jesus. And when Paul had laid his hands upon them, the Holy Ghost came on them; and they spake with tongues, and prophesied. And all the men were about twelve (Acts 19:1-7).

THE DIFFERENCE IN CONTRAST

There is a difference between being *born of the Spirit* and being *baptized in the Spirit*. At salvation, life is imparted to someone who was once dead. As the apostle Paul revealed to the saints in Colossae, "You were dead because of your sins and because your sinful nature was not yet cut away. Then God made you alive with Christ, for he forgave all our sins" (Col. 2:13 NLT).

We were dead in sin and separated from God, but through the new birth, the life of God was imparted and deposited into our spirits. Now if life was imparted through salvation, in the baptism in the Holy Spirit, power is imparted to the believer who was previously weak and powerless. This endowment of power renders the believer fit for service to God. That is why Jesus specifically said, "…but tarry ye in the city of Jerusalem, until ye **be endued with power from on high**" (Luke 24:49). Dr. Luke reiterates the same message in his second treatise to Theophillus:

> *And, being assembled together with them, commanded them that they should not depart from Jerusalem, but wait for the promise of the Father, which, saith he, ye have heard of me. For John truly baptized with water; but* **ye shall be baptized with the Holy Ghost not many days hence** *(Acts 1:4-5).*

Therefore, according to the Scripture, every believer needs this endowment and clothing of power. We obtain authority and "right to be," which in Greek is *exousia*—sons of God—at the new birth (see John 1:12), but we receive power and *ability to act*, which in Greek is *dunamis*, after the Holy Spirit comes upon us and we are filled with the Holy Spirit. (Acts 1:8). A simple way to remember this is that in the new birth the Holy Spirit came and indwelt you, but in the baptism of the Holy Spirit, the same indwelling Spirit comes upon you.

CONTINUATIONIST OR CESSATIONIST

Those of us who believe in *glossolalia* and the supernatural gifts of the Spirit are still functioning today as they were in the Book of Acts are deemed to be Continuationists or Continualists. Those who oppose this view and teach that tongues and the gifts are passed away and were only intended for a season as foundation for the New Testament Church transitioning from the Old Covenant to the New Covenant are known as Cessationists. They are the proponents of *"All these ended when the last apostle died. It is not for today."* Is this concept scriptural? No! No! No! A thousand times...no! Now, I am not insinuating in any way that the people who believe in this notion are not saved or that they do no love the Lord or are insincere. They may be sincere but they are sincerely wrong! These are born-again believers who are on their way to Heaven. They are our brothers and sisters in Christ. They are just as saved as those of us who are considered as Continuationists. It is just simply that they do not believe that *glossolalia* and *charismata* are for us today! Every name that I choose to mention in this book is not meant to be critical or as a put down. It is to show you a glimpse of the history of cessationism. I am in no way defaming the person or group in question, but I am coming against what I believe is wrong, or doctrine of devils keeping the people of God away from His best.

WHERE DID ALL THIS CESSATIONISM START?

Although cessationism proponents have always been around (such as the Sadducees, Judaism against Jesus, early Christian fathers against the Jews, John Calvin, to name a few), B.B. Warfield, born in Lexington, Kentucky, on November 5, 1851, a professor of theology at Princeton Seminary from 1887 to 1921, was undoubtedly the voice of the first modern cessationist to develop the theory that glossolalia and the apostles were inextricable and that charismata passed away with the apostolic age. Benjamin Warfield was a critic of much religious revivalism that was popular in America at the time. He believed that the teachings and experience of this movement (Pentecostalism) were too subjective, and therefore, too shallow for deep Christian faith. His book, *Counterfeit Miracles*, written in 1918, was pivotal and became the flag bearer for cessationism against miracles after the time of the apostles. Warfield's argument was that the special charismata were *"distinctively for the authentication of the apostles."*[1]

The 1917 *Scofield Reference Bible*, an extremely impactful Bible, also endorsed cessationism, which had significant repercussions in the Church world. However, in reading the responses to questions posed to Paul in First Corinthians chapter 12 through chapter 14, you will discover that Paul himself was a proponent of *glossolalia* and *charismata* gifts. He strongly defended tongues and the proper use of the gifts within the church in these three chapters. In the fourteenth chapter of First Corinthians, Paul emphatically declared that he himself was a practitioner of tongues; but at the same time, he addressed the abuse and improper use of the gift as well as encouraged the believer to desire the supernatural. So Paul was a Continuationist unlike modern and reformed theologians.

I believe that cessationism is nothing but a deceptive ploy of satan to keep the Church weak and dead. Satan loves dead churches with dead preachers preaching dead sermons to dead people, but he loathes seeing dead believers and churches transformed, set on fire and the blowing of winds of revival. It is, therefore, instinctive to his insidious nature to promote the demonic doctrine suggesting that this phenomenon *is not for today*. If satan had his way, speaking in tongues would not have been for *any* day, *any* dispensation, or season. Much has been said against tongues, Pentecostalism, and Charismatics—and much of it very detrimental. Famous ministers of old and entire denominations vehemently denounced the movement, the people, and its practice. A famed minister went as far as labeling Pentecostalism as *"the last vomit of satan."*

Now let's look at some of the cessationist objections and arguments against the baptism with the Holy Spirit with the evidence of speaking in other tongues.

Objection 1: Tongues were solely for the early Church dispensation and not for us today.

Anti-tongue theologians propagated this belief and have made it a doctrine suggesting that "Tongues is not for today; it ended when the last apostle died." Millions in the Church world have bought into this nefarious fabrication, but thank God there are multiplied millions who have rejected this opinion. The Holy Scripture, which is our manual for life, does not concur with this belief. Let us look at what the Word says:

> But Peter, standing up with the eleven, lifted up his voice, and said unto them, Ye men of Judaea, and all ye that dwell at Jerusalem, be this known unto you, and hearken to my words: For these are not drunken, as ye suppose, seeing it is but the third hour of the day. **But this is that which was spoken by the prophet Joel; And it shall come to pass in the last days**, saith God, I will pour out of My Spirit upon all flesh: and your sons and your daughters shall prophesy, and your young men shall see visions, and your old men shall dream dreams: And on My servants and on My handmaidens I will pour out in those days of My Spirit; and they shall prophesy (Acts 2:14-18).

> Then Peter said unto them, Repent, and be baptized every one of you in the name of Jesus Christ for the remission of sins, and ye shall receive the gift of the Holy Ghost. **For the promise is unto you, and to your children, and to all that are afar off, even as many as the Lord our God shall call** (Acts 2:38-39).

> And it shall come to pass afterward, that I will pour out My Spirit upon all flesh; and your sons and your daughters shall prophesy, your old men shall dream dreams, your young men shall see visions: And also upon the servants and upon the handmaids in those days will I pour out My Spirit (Joel 2:28-29).

Peter, in his first sermon, compared the prophecy of the prophet Joel being fulfilled to the phenomenon that occurred on the day of Pentecost. This prophecy was fulfilled on the day of Pentecost, and we are living in the reality of this fulfillment. We are still living in the last days, and this prophecy is still in vogue. Peter validates this point when he says, "For the promise is unto you, and to your children, and to all that are afar off, even as many as the Lord our God shall call" (Acts 2:39).

Tongues and the gifts of the Spirit are for us today. These gifts did not pass away with the apostles. If that were the case, then these gifts would be known as the gifts of the apostles and not the gifts of the Spirit. Paul also stated, "But the manifestation of the Spirit is given to every man to profit withal" (1 Cor. 12:7). Notice these words, *"given to every man."* It is not just for the apostles but for every person in the Church. Trying to say that we live in a different dispensation than the early Church is ludicrous. The early Church and the current Church are in the last days and what is known as the Church Age. Let's bear in mind what Paul pointed out in his letter to Corinth, "And **God hath set some in the church,** first apostles...after that miracles, then gifts of healings...**diversities of tongues**" (1 Cor. 12:28). This is very clear and concise: God has set in the church diversities of tongues. Tongues are an institution of God for the Church.

We must welcome speaking in tongues and accept it. Solomon in his wisdom said, "The thing that hath been, it is that which shall be; and that which is done is that which shall be done: and there is no new thing under the sun" (Eccles. 1:9). A little study and comprehension of the Book of First Corinthians will enable you to know that this epistle was a question and answer session. Paul was responding to questions the Corinthian church had. The *tongues-is-not-for-us-today* argument is no new thing. It was prevalent in the days of Paul too, and there were doubters who wanted to forbid tongues in church just as today. But Paul silenced these troublemakers when he said, "Do not forbid speaking in tongues" (1 Cor. 14:39), and "I would that ye all spake with tongues....I thank my God, I speak with tongues more than ye all" (1 Cor. 14:5,18). These are not the words of a man who was against tongues and was discouraging people from this great blessing. Here are some facts from the Scriptures to prove and validate that we are still in the dispensation of the last days, just as Peter and Paul:

> *This know also, that in the last days perilous times shall come* (2 Timothy 3:1).

God, who at sundry times and in divers manners spake in time past unto the fathers by the prophets,Hath in these last days spoken unto us by his Son, whom he hath appointed heir of all things, by whom also he made the worlds (Hebrews 1:1-2).

Forasmuch as ye know that ye were not redeemed with corruptible things, as silver and gold, from your vain conversation received by tradition from your fathers; But with the precious blood of Christ, as of a lamb without blemish and without spot: Who verily was foreordained before the foundation of the world, but was manifest in these last times for you (1 Peter 1:18-20).

Little children, it is the last time: and as ye have heard that antichrist shall come, even now are there many antichrists; whereby we know that it is the last time (1 John 2:18).

But, beloved, remember ye the words which were spoken before of the apostles of our Lord Jesus Christ; How that they told you there should be mockers in the last time, who should walk after their own ungodly lusts (Jude 1:17-18).

We can see in all of the references above that we are living in the last days, even as the early Church lived and experienced perilous times. Tongues were and are for the Church Age. It has not ceased!

When Did the Charismata and Glossolalia Cease According to Cessationists?

My study over the years reveals that Cessationists are divided into different groups. Here is how we can define the four different types and beliefs:

Concentric Cessationists state and believe that the miraculous gifts have indeed ceased in the mainstream church and evangelized areas but appear in unreached areas as an aid to spreading the Gospel.

Classical Cessationists believe that the sign gifts, such as prophecy, healing, and speaking in tongues ceased with the apostles and the finishing of the canon of Scripture. They only served as launching pads for the spreading of the Gospel, as affirmations of God's revelation. However, these cessationists do believe that God still occasionally does miracles today, such as healings or divine guidance, so long as these *miracles* do not accredit new doctrine or add to the New Testament canon.

Full Cessationists argue that along with no miraculous gifts, there are also no miracles performed by God today.

Consistent Cessationists believe that not only were the miraculous gifts for the establishment of the first-century Church, but that the fivefold ministry found in Ephesians 4 was also a transitional institution. This means there are no more apostles or prophets, but also no more pastors, teachers, or evangelists.

I believe that all of these four beliefs do not line up with the Scriptures and go against what Jude stated, "...exhort you that ye should earnestly contend for the faith which was once delivered unto the saints" (see Jude 3). The cessationism doctrine does not sound like "contending for the faith" that was once delivered to the saints but resembles another gospel that Paul warned about, "I marvel that ye are so soon removed from him that called you into the grace of Christ unto another gospel" (Gal. 1:6). The word *another* is *heteros* and means "different and one not of the same nature, form, class, kind." So, removing the supernatural, the charismata, and glossolalia out of the church does not line up with the faith that was once delivered and with the Great Commission. It is a different quality *gospel*. To further complicate matters, the Cessationists cannot agree on the cessation dates. Here are some dates they suppose the gifts ceased, and that is naming a few:

- A.D. 70 with the destruction of the Jewish temple.
- A.D. 96 when John wrote the last book of the Bible, Revelation.
- After the last apostle, John, died.
- After the last disciple of one of the 12 apostles died.

38

- After the children of the disciples of Jesus passed away.

- After the last disciple to whom the apostles conferred a gift died.

- After the apostolic age, around A.D. 150.

- After the canon of Scripture.

- After a complete Holy Bible was printed in Greek or Latin.

- After the Bible was translated into German or English.

- After the Authorized King James Version was made available to the masses of people.

Objection 2: Tongues have ceased due to the canon of Scripture

Another verse Cessasionist believers use to discredit tongues is First Corinthians 13:8-10 and is the apex of their belief: "Charity never faileth: but whether there be prophecies, they shall fail; whether there be tongues, they shall cease; whether there be knowledge, it shall vanish away. For we know in part, and we prophesy in part. But when that which is perfect is come, then that which is in part shall be done away."

Whether a person is a Continualist or a Cessationist, the one thing they agree on is that these gifts will cease and be done away with. The problem is the timing of the cessation. Evidently, Paul believed this, and referred to a future time when these gifts will cease, "...when that which is perfect comes...." This simply means these gifts were in effect and operating in Paul's days and that the time of their cessation was a future event for him. The bone of contention is in whether the gifts mentioned have ceased prior to our time, or whether they are still operative for us, as they were for Paul. So when would they cease according to Paul? Let's look at what he actually says:

Charity never faileth: but whether there be prophecies, they shall fail; whether there be tongues, they shall cease; whether there be knowledge, it shall vanish away. For we know in part, and we prophesy in part. But when that which is perfect is come, then that which is in part shall be done away. When I was a child, I spake as a child, I understood as a child, I thought as a child: but when I became a man, I put away childish things. For now we see through a glass, darkly; but then face to face: now I know in part; but then shall I know even as also I am known (1 Corinthians 13:8-12).

Paul gave three specific descriptions of the point in time in which tongues will cease:

1. When that which is perfect is come.

2. When we see face to face.

3. When we know, even as we are known.

Anti-tongues proponents argue that, *"When that which is perfect is come"* was fulfilled when the last apostle wrote the last book of the Bible and the time of the completion of the canon of Scripture. Of course, we believe in the canon of the Scripture and its infallibility, but that has nothing to do with "when that is perfect is come." I believe that the word, *perfect*, refers to Christ and not to the Scripture. This is further supported as Paul said that we would see "face to face." In other words, "when that which is perfect is come" has a face. There is no face on my Bible, but Jesus Christ has a face. The word *perfect* refers to our Lord, Master, Redeemer, High Priest, and Savior: "And being made perfect, He became the author of eternal salvation." (See Hebrews 5:9.) Then Paul wrote that we would know as well as we are known. I don't know as well as I am known. When will we know as we are known? Our knowledge of all things will become perfect at Christ's Second Coming, when corruption takes on incorruption and mortality will put on immortality—when every believer will put on the glorified body.

Paul concluded that tongues would continue until perfection (being Christ) came and until we see Him face to face, with our knowledge being entirely complete. Then there would be no further need for the gift of tongues. The cessationist argument that tongues and prophecy have passed away is not valid for the simple reason that if that were the case, then knowledge should have vanished too.

The irrationality of claiming that the *"when that which is perfect is come"* alludes to the canon of Scripture would imply that we today see face to face, whereas Paul and the other apostles were looking through a dark glass. This also conveys the idea that Paul, Peter, and John knew in part and that we know the full part. I believe this is incorrect. When that which is perfect is come refers to the coming of the Lord, and these gifts will cease when the King of kings returns.

> *I thank my God always on your behalf, for the grace of God which is given you by Jesus Christ; That in every thing ye are enriched by him, in all utterance, and in all knowledge; Even as the testimony of Christ was confirmed in you:* **So that ye come behind in no gift; waiting for the coming of our Lord Jesus Christ: Who shall also confirm you unto the end,** *that ye may be blameless in the day of our Lord Jesus Christ* (1 Corinthians 1:4-8).

Objection 3: Tongues, the charismata gifts, signs and wonders were only to confirm and authenticate the apostles. According to cessationism, this was the crowning sign of their divine commission.

> *How shall we escape, if we neglect so great salvation; which at the first began to be spoken by the Lord, and was confirmed unto us by them that heard Him; God also bearing* **them** *witness, both with signs and wonders, and with divers miracles, and gifts of the Holy Ghost, according to His own will?* (Hebrews 2:3-4)

The irrationality of using this verse in the second chapter of Hebrews as ground to claim that God only used miracles to confirm the apostles is exegetically invalid. Notice the word *them* in the above verse is bolded. As mentioned before, any time you see an italicized (bolded) word in the King James Authorized version, it simply means it was not in the original literal Greek text but was inserted at the discretion of the translators, supposedly to help the reader. This supposition proves to be most unhelpful as it takes away from what the verse is saying. So take out the word *them* and this is how the verse reads, "…at the first began to be **spoken by the Lord,** and was confirmed unto us by them that heard him; *God also bearing…witness, both with signs and wonders, and with divers miracles, and gifts of* the Holy Ghost, according to His own will?" God confirmed that which was first spoken of the Lord. God was confirming His word with signs following.

There are two references with the word *them* added to the subject of signs and wonders that should not be there. One is in Hebrews, as we have observed; and the other is in the last chapter of the Gospel of Mark.

> *And these signs shall follow them that believe; In My name shall they cast out devils; they shall speak with new tongues; They shall take up serpents; and if they drink any deadly thing, it shall not hurt them; they shall lay hands on the sick, and they shall recover. So then after the Lord had spoken unto them, He was received up into heaven, and sat on the right hand of God. And they went forth, and preached every where, the Lord working with* **them**, *and confirming the word with signs following. Amen* (Mark 16:17-20).

Once again, the word them was put there, and it completely takes away from what the verse is saying. When you take out the word *them*, the verse reads as follows, "And they went forth, and preached every where, the Lord working with and confirming the word with signs following. Amen" (Mark 16:20). The Lord works with and confirms the Word that is preached with signs following. God works with His Word. God confirms His Word, not the apostles. Can you see the ruse of the wicked one here? If you allow the word *them*, it would say ...*the Lord was working and confirming the apostles.* That is not the case! God works and confirms His Word. Faith comes by hearing and hearing the Word of God (see Rom. 10:17). As Paul states, when faith comes, substance shows up (see Heb. 11:1). The Word brings the substance of signs. Let us look once again at the verse in Hebrews:

> *How shall we escape, if we neglect so great salvation; which at the first began to be spoken by the Lord, and was confirmed unto us by them that heard Him; God also bearing* **them** *witness, both with signs and wonders, and*

with divers miracles, and gifts of the Holy Ghost, according to His own will? (Hebrews 2:3-4)

Their Deduction From Hebrews 2

This is what cessationists conclude from the two verses in Hebrews:

- It was the apostles who heard the Lord.
- The miracles, gifts, sign and wonders, validated and confirmed their apostolic ministry.
- The miracles, gifts, signs and wonders, were only done through the apostles.
- Upon completion of their apostolic ministry, the miracles, gifts, and supernatural elements of ministry and the church ended; for it was only proof of apostolic ministry's authenticity.

Do their deductions line up with Scriptures? Absolutely not! Here are four answers to their deductions. First, there were more people than the foundational apostles who heard the Lord; and that would include, to name one example, the seventy who were commissioned by the Lord to heal the sick and cast out devils. Second, as already mentioned, the confirmation was not geared toward the apostles, but God was confirming the Word preached. Here are some verses to confirm this:

Long time therefore abode they speaking boldly in the Lord, which gave testimony unto the word of His grace, and granted signs and wonders to be done by their hands (Acts 14:3).

Now I say that Jesus Christ was a minister of the circumcision for the truth of God, to confirm the promises made unto the fathers (Romans 15:8).

Wherein God, willing more abundantly to shew unto the heirs of promise the immutability of His counsel, confirmed it by an oath (Hebrews 6:17).

And this I say, that the covenant, that was confirmed before of God in Christ, the law, which was four hundred and thirty years after, cannot disannul, that it should make the promise of none effect (Galatians 3:17).

Third, to say that miracles, gifts, signs and wonders, were only done through the apostles is preposterous. Ananias, who laid hands on Paul to receive his sight, was described as a certain disciple.

> *And there was a certain disciple at Damascus, named Ananias; and to him said the Lord in a vision, Ananias. And he said, Behold, I am here, Lord...And hath seen in a vision a man named Ananias coming in, and putting his hand on him, that he might receive his sight. And Ananias went his way, and entered into the house; and putting his hands on him said, Brother Saul, the Lord, even Jesus, that appeared unto thee in the way as thou camest, hath sent me, that thou mightest receive thy sight, and be filled with the Holy Ghost. And immediately there fell from his eyes as it had been scales: and he received sight forthwith, and arose, and was baptized* (Acts 9:10,12,17-18).

This completely discredits the theory that miracles and signs were only done by the apostles. Ananias was a disciple! The Greek word for "disciple" is *mathetes*, and it means "a learner and pupil." Ananias was not a teacher or apostle. How about Stephen? He was no apostle but a deacon, one who served tables, and yet he walked in signs and wonders.

> *And the saying pleased the whole multitude: and they chose Stephen, a man full of faith and of the Holy Ghost...And Stephen, full of faith and power, did great wonders and miracles among the people* (Acts 6:5,8).

Here is the secret to Stephen's signs and wonders ministry! He was a man full of faith, the Holy Ghost, and power! That would explain where the cessationist is missing it. You cannot talk down signs and wonders and have a supernatural ministry. If you disdain faith, you will attract doubt and unbelief.

To further answer this erroneous claim of miracles only done through apostles, let us look at the Corinthian and Galatian churches. Paul told the Corinthian church, a bunch of unruly lot, "I thank my

God always on your behalf, for the grace of God which is given you by Jesus Christ; That in every thing ye are enriched by Him, in all utterance, and in all knowledge; Even as the testimony of Christ was confirmed in you: So that ye come behind in no gift; waiting for the coming of our Lord Jesus Christ" (1 Cor. 1:4-7). To the Galatian church Paul asked, "He therefore that ministereth to you the Spirit, and worketh miracles among you, doeth He it by the works of the law, or by the hearing of faith?" (Gal. 3:5). The requirement for miracles, signs and wonders is faith, not apostleship.

Fourth, and finally, skeptics prescribe to the fallacy that miracles passed away with the completion of the apostolic ministries. This is outlandish! If that were the case, then these gifts should have been called *the gifts of the apostles*. The last time we checked, it was called the gifts of the Spirit and the manifestations of the Spirit. In addition, we need to consider the third chapter of Hebrews which states, "Wherefore, holy brethren, partakers of the heavenly calling, consider the Apostle and High Priest of our profession, Christ Jesus" (Heb. 3:1).

Jesus Christ is the Apostle of our confession, and He is not dead. His ministry is still here today. Miracles, signs and wonders are for us today as the Apostle Jesus Christ is alive forevermore. To cap it, we simply need to remember what Jesus said, "And these signs shall follow them that believe..." (Mark 16:17). Jesus did not say, "And these signs will specially and specifically follow the apostles." Signs, gifts, healings, and tongues follow the believer, and thank the Lord the apostles were believing believers.

Objection 4: Tongues and the charismata gifts were foundational in addition to being dispensational and not personal.

> *And are built upon the foundation of the apostles and prophets, Jesus Christ Himself being the chief corner stone* (Ephesians 2:20).

Cessationists quote Ephesians 2:20 to justify the "foundational and dispensational" opinion. Yes the Church was indeed built on Christ, apostles, and prophets, but this verse is in no way suggesting that any of these ministry offices or the charismata stopped after any period. If anything, it is saying the contrary—that the ministries of prophets and apostles continue, as you see in Ephesians 4:11-13, "And He gave some, apostles; and some, prophets; and some, evangelists; and some, pastors and teachers; For the perfecting of the saints, for the work of the ministry, for the edifying of the body of Christ: **Till we all come in the unity of the faith, and of the knowledge of the Son of God, unto a perfect man, unto the measure of the stature of the fulness of Christ.**" This prophetic proclamation will only be fulfilled and completed when the Master returns.

Objection 5: Tongues were for preaching the Gospel to foreigners.

Other theologians have said that tongues is an ability given to preach the Gospel in the language of foreigners citing the second chapter of Acts.

> *And they were all filled with the Holy Ghost, and began to speak with other tongues, as the Spirit gave them utterance. And there were dwelling at Jerusalem Jews, devout men, out of every nation under heaven. Now when this was noised abroad, the multitude came together, and were confounded, because that every man heard them speak in his own language. And they were all amazed and marvelled, saying one to another, Behold, are not all these which speak Galilaeans? And how hear we every man in our own tongue, wherein we were born?...we do hear them speak in our tongues the wonderful works of God"* (Acts 2:4-8,11).

This theory is also unsubstantiated, as none of those who heard the disciples speaking in other tongues were saved until Peter spoke or preached in his own tongue. If this theory was credible, then the tongues that Peter and the disciples spoke would be old languages that already existed. There is no record that any of the apostles or the 120 gathered in the Upper Room ever preached the Gospel in tongues. Not one record! It never happened at Pentecost as the Cessationist claims. The multitude who had come and gathered in Jerusalem that day did not say to the disciples after they heard them in tongues, "We have heard you concerning Jesus Christ. He is the only way, the truth, and the life, and now we accept His substitutionary sacrifice." No; here is what the crowd said, "We do hear them speak in our tongues the wonderful works of God" (Acts 2:11). As a matter of fact, it was not a case of the 120 disciples going after the crowd, but it was the multitude in Jerusalem that came toward them due to the noise they were making praying in tongues. Here's the fact from the verse: "**And there were dwelling at Jerusalem Jews, devout men, out of every nation under heaven. Now when this was noised abroad, the multitude came together, and were confounded, because that every man heard them speak in his own language**...And how hear we every man in our own tongue, wherein we were born?...we do hear them speak in our tongues the wonderful works of God" (Acts 2:5-6,8,11). The 120 disciples were just there, audibly and roaringly praising God in other tongues, which alarmed the multitude who rushed to them and distinguished different languages.

As I have already mentioned, not one of the 120 were preaching the Gospel or testifying in tongues. On the day of Pentecost Peter did not preach in tongues, but he preached in his own native language the way of salvation and then three thousand souls were added to the Church. Tongues were not used to preach the Gospel. What kinds of tongues were the disciples uttering? They were praying and praising God in spirit, which is the same thing Paul said, "I will pray with the spirit, and I will pray with the understanding also. I will sing with the spirit, and I will sing with the understanding also" (1 Cor. 14:15). Paul, and all those before and after him, prayed in tongues and worshiped God in tongues.

> *And these signs shall follow them that believe; In My name shall they cast out devils; they shall speak with new tongues* (Mark 16:17).

> *But in the church I would rather speak five intelligible words to instruct others than ten thousand words in a tongue* (1 Corinthians 14:19 NIV).

The abuse of the Corinthian church was the fact they would do everything in tongues. They would begin the service by greeting in tongues then proceed with the praise and worship in tongues. Then the Word will be ministered in tongues. Clearly, you can see the confusion that would bring in the church. Preaching the Gospel or ministration is to be done in the tongue that is known among the hearers.

Paul admonished it to the Corinthians, and Peter showed it on the day of Pentecost. Those who spoke in tongues at Cornelius's house and the Ephesians of Acts 19 all spoke in tongues or prayed in tongues without foreigners around to hear.

> *And it came to pass, that, while Apollos was at Corinth, Paul having passed through the upper coasts came to Ephesus: and finding certain disciples, he said unto them, Have ye received the Holy Ghost since ye believed? And they said unto him, We have not so much as heard whether there be any Holy Ghost. And he said unto them, Unto what then were ye baptized? And they said, Unto John's baptism. Then said Paul, John verily baptized with the baptism of repentance, saying unto the people, that they should believe on Him which should come after him, that is, on Christ Jesus. When they heard this, they were baptized in the name of the Lord Jesus. And when Paul had laid his hands upon them, the Holy Ghost came on them; and they spake with tongues, and prophesied. And all the men were about twelve* (Acts 19:1-7).

Objection 6: "Do all speak with tongues?"

Cessationists always love to quote the following verse as their emblem of pride. You do not have to be a long-term believer before running into people who believe this and use this particular verse of Scripture to vehemently defend and convince themselves that *glosso-lalia* is not for us today and much worse, *that it is of the devil!* Here is the verse in question:

> *Are all apostles? are all prophets? are all teachers? are all workers of miracles? Have all the gifts of healing? do all speak with tongues? do all interpret?* (1 Corinthians 12:29-30)

Glossolallia critics have forcefully pounded that not all Christians can have the gift of tongues and that Pentecostals and Charismatics are wrong for saying so. In one sense, they are right as Paul clearly says that not all have the gift of speaking in tongues. The Greek interlinear of the New Testament states it clearly when it reads, "Do all speak in tongues? No." (See First Corinthians 12:30.) This is emphatic! Our first impression would be that the anti-tongues group is right and that there is a discrepancy in these zealous emotional Pentecostals' and Charismatics' advocacy of *tongues for all*. However, with a little study and rightly dividing the Word as Paul instructed, one will see and understand the context of the text to know there is a distinction and difference between the ministry gift of utterance in tongues and tongues as a private devotional prayer language. Glossolalia is separated into two distinct categories. To give a proper answer to this question, one has to go back to the very beginning of this particular twelfth chapter of Corinthians. "Now concerning spiritual gifts, brethren, I would not have you ignorant" (1 Cor. 12:1).

There are several words for the word *gift* in the New Testament, and they are *phanerosis*, *charismata*, *dorea*, and *domata*. In First Corinthians 12:1, the word employed is *pneumatikos*, and it means "that which entails spiritual matters and the supernatural." Once again if you look at your Authorized Version, you will notice that the word *gifts* is italicized meaning it was not in the original text but was put there at the discretion of the translators to help us which in this case as in so many other cases did not. You see, this chapter and the following two chapters of this epistle deal with more than just the gifts but also with the ministries, motives, and the mechanics of the supernatural in the make up of the church. It also talks about tongues as a prayer language and tongues as a gift of utterance, coupled with interpretation to edify the church. There is a big difference between the two.

In this particular verse, Paul is referring to public ministry gifts that are manifested in the church. He is not talking about tongues as the initial sign of the baptism in the Spirit or as a private, devotional, prayer language. The prayer language is for "personal edification," whereas the gift of utterance is used for "public ministry." Carefully look at the language Paul uses concerning speaking in tongues in his Corinthian's epistle. He uses the expressions, **divers** kinds of tongues and **diversities** of tongues, meaning different kinds, thus signifying *not the usual*. (See First Corinthians 12.) The usual or norm would be the prayer language, but the *gift of utterance* of tongues, of which Paul is speaking of here, is the same as eight other gifts which, obviously, all do not have. The usual kind of speaking in tongues is a language no man understands or interprets. So when Paul

asks the question, "Do all speak in tongues?" he was, in effect, referring to the public manifestation of the gift of tongues which enables a
person gifted in interpretation to speak out the meaning of the tongue
to edify the church congregation. It is evident that not everybody
walks in that gift just as not everybody can claim within a church set
up that they are apostles, prophets, or teachers. So Paul was in no way
referring to the personal, devotional prayer language of tongues.

Objection 7: Tongues is self-centered and egocentric not benefit-ing the Church body.

> He that speaketh in an unknown tongue edifieth himself;
> but he that prophesieth edifieth the church (1 Corinthians
> 14:4).

Another stinging criticism from the anti-tongues crew is that
tongues are only for self-edification and not for the edification of the
church. Therefore, it is egocentric, prideful, and does not reflect the
virtue of Christ. That sounds like humility but in reality this is nothing but false humility at the highest level of hypocrisy, masquerading
a cover up for pride. There is nowhere in the Word where Paul or
any other apostles were against personal edification. See what Jude
said, "But you beloved, building up yourselves on your most holy
faith, praying in the Holy Ghost" (Jude 1:20). Paul also stated,
"And now, brethren, I commend you to God, and to the word of
His grace, which is able to build you up, and to give you an inheri-
tance among all them which are sanctified" (Acts 20:32). Everything
that we do, whether it is reading the Bible, prayer, or even attending
church, are for our edification. Paul was not in any way denigrating
self-edification through tongues but showing us a contrast between
the believer's edification and the Body's edification. There is a time
and place for the personal use of tongues, which edifies the believer;
and there is a place for prophecy, which builds the Body.

Objection 8: Tongues are not for us today as Paul said he would rather speak five words in understanding than ten thousand words in unknown tongue.

> Yet in the church I had rather speak five words with my
> understanding, that by my voice I might teach others

also, than ten thousand words in an unknown tongue
(1 Corinthians 14:19).

Those who are anti-tongues proponents love to take this verse and quote it as to why they don't do tongues. Paul, who already declared that he spoke in tongues more than anyone, was in no way demeaning tongues but was addressing an abuse of it. The church in Corinth had become unbalanced in their worship services. As already mentioned, they were holding services in tongues and ministering in tongues. Paul was referring to teaching of the Word, "**Yet in the church** I had rather speak five words with my understanding, **that by my voice I might teach...**" (1 Cor. 14:19). Teaching enlightens or gives understanding, whereas tongues bypass the understanding. So the context of this verse has to do with preaching and teaching in corporate worship, and you do not do that in tongues. Paul was concerned about the edification of the church. Tongues would only edify the person but not the corporate Body. Paul was not downplaying tongues. He was only explaining to the Corinthians that in corporate worship, the edification of the whole Body is imperative.

There are people who wonder why we pray and praise in tongues in a church service asking whether this is in direct opposition to Paul's instruction on orderly worship. The simple answer is that Paul was not confronting the issue of speaking in tongues collectively, but was giving clear and concise guidance to those who want to address the congregation to do it in known tongue rather than in tongues. We can corporately pray and praise God in tongues, but when we are addressing the congregation, we do so in our language. However, if there is an utterance of the gift of tongues, it must be followed by interpretation. Otherwise, the speaker of the message in tongues should keep quiet or pray to interpret himself.

Objection 9: Tongues is not for us today for it is the least gift.

And God hath set some in the church, first apostles, secondarily prophets, thirdly teachers, after that miracles, then gifts of healings, helps, governments, diversities of tongues (1 Corinthians 12:28).

Here is the squabble that opponents of continualism use to defend their stance, "Tongues are mentioned last in First Corinthians 12:28.

Therefore, they are the least of the gifts." This insinuates that tongues are of such little value that mature Christians do not need to bother with this *inferior* gift. The order of how the list was written was not necessarily an indication of importance. If we used the same interpretation for First Corinthians 13:13 in which Paul tells us, "And now these three remain: faith, hope and love. But the greatest of these is love" (NIV), then faith and not love should be the greatest. In spite of the fact that love is listed last, yet Paul said it is the greatest. So we cannot use this kind of interpretation with the Corinthians list too.

Objection 10: New Tongues means no cussing.

This is laughable! Another lame excuse that has been propagated by theologians who are anti-tongues is to say that new tongues meant that there won't be any cussing in your mouth. It is true that there should not be any profanity in the mouth of the believer, but this is not a "new thing."

Objection 11: Tongues is based on experience and is nonsensical emotionalism.

Cessationists declare that those who profess to have the baptism of the Holy Spirit with praying in tongues and believe in the charismata gifts are only basing such phenomenon on an experience and not the Bible. Others have said, "This is nothing but hype of emotions!" Well, we can turn the table around and say that Cessationists are basing their lack of supernatural power upon their experiences or lack of experiences, to be more precise. In effect, they are rejecting the people's experiences because of their lack of experiences. Paul clearly expresses in his letter to the Romans, "And patience, experience; and experience, hope" (Rom. 5:4). Experience releases hope. The reason Cessationists do not have any hope of the supernatural is because they have never experienced it. Their idea is, *If I did not experience it, then in no way can your experience be valid.*

Cessationism puts God in a box and limits the God who is unlimited. According to the author of the Book of Hebrews, "Jesus Christ the same yesterday, and to day, and for ever" (Heb. 13:8), and the prophet Malachi revealed, "I am the Lord and I change not" (see Mal.

3:6). Cessationism is based on intellectual unbelief and is a pitiful excuse for a lack of power. The disciples could have used the same excuse when faced with the epileptic boy in the Gospel of Luke.

> *When Jesus had called the Twelve together, He gave them power and authority to drive out all demons and to cure diseases, and He sent them out to preach the kingdom of God and to heal the sick. He told them: "Take nothing for the journey—no staff, no bag, no bread, no money, no extra tunic. Whatever house you enter, stay there until you leave that town. If people do not welcome you, shake the dust off your feet when you leave their town, as a testimony against them." So they set out and went from village to village, preaching the gospel and healing people everywhere* (Luke 9:1-6 NIV).

Please note that the disciples could do the commands of Jesus in the sixth verse above and look at the conclusion, "When the apostles returned, they reported to Jesus what they had done" (Luke 9:10). Then an interesting turn of events occurred in the same chapter a few verses below.

> *And it came to pass, that on the next day, when they were come down from the hill, much people met Him. And, behold, a man of the company cried out, saying, Master, I beseech thee, look upon my son: for he is mine only child. And, lo, a spirit taketh him, and he suddenly crieth out; and it teareth him that he foameth again, and bruising him hardly departeth from him. **And I besought Thy disciples to cast him out; and they could not.** And Jesus answering said, O faithless and perverse generation, how long shall I be with you, and suffer you? Bring thy son hither. And as he was yet a coming, the devil threw him down, and tare him. And Jesus rebuked the unclean spirit, and healed the child, and delivered him again to his father. And they were all amazed at the mighty power of God. But while they wondered every one at all things which Jesus did…* (Luke 9:37-43).

Notice these words, "And I besought Thy disciples to cast him out; and they could not" (Luke 9:40). Something expired between verse

THE POWER of PRAYING in TONGUES

ten and verse forty where they could not do what they had done before. The miraculous that flowed beforehand was now not operating. They could have used all kinds of excuses and been Cessasionists. They could have said, "This was two weeks ago or a month ago, and now these gifts are not for us today." No, they did not do that! The Word says, "After Jesus had gone indoors, His disciples asked Him privately, 'Why couldn't we drive it out?'" (Mark 9:28 NIV). They realized the problem was themselves. In fact, the Lord called it unbelief, which is exactly what cessationism is. Cessationism is not the banner of truth that it has portrayed.

The dilemma that Cessationists face today is in their stating that they are sticklers for the truth. Then the same effort to seek truth must be applied honestly to glossolalia and charismata. The disdain, distortion, and deception in regard to continuationism must be confronted and eradicated from within their own camp. Our Lord said, "Your tradition has made the Word of God of no effect" (see Mark 7:13). Actually, this was a response and rebuke to the Pharisees and Scribes.

> *Howbeit in vain do they worship me, teaching for doctrines the commandments of men. For laying aside the commandment of God, ye hold the tradition of men, as the washing of pots and cups: and many other such like things ye do. And he said unto them, Full well ye reject the commandment of God, that ye may keep your own tradition. For Moses said, Honour thy father and thy mother; and, Whoso curseth father or mother, let him die the death: But ye say, If a man shall say to his father or mother, It is Corban, that is to say, a gift, by whatsoever thou mightest be profited by me; he shall be free. And ye suffer him no more to do ought for his father or his mother; Making the word of God of none effect through your tradition, which ye have delivered: and many such like things do ye (Mark 7:7-13).*

I want you to notice the words of the Master (see Mark 7:7-8):

- *Teaching for doctrines the commandments of men.*

- *For laying aside the commandment of God, ye hold the tradition of men...many other such like things ye do.*

- *Full well ye reject the commandment of God, that ye may keep your own tradition.*

- *Making the word of God of none effect through your tradition, which ye have delivered: and many such like things do ye.*

In essence, that is what cessationism is. It is not validated by the Scripture but is a tradition of humankind rejecting the commands of Jesus, the Great and Chief Shepherd of the Church. Cessationism is rebellion against God's definite decrees and idolatry in the sense that they worship a theoretical intellectual dogma, thereby making it the golden calf above God. It is taking the words of humanity above the decrees of God. The Scripture clearly says, "Let God be true and every man a liar" (see Rom. 3:4). Cessationism depicts God as a liar. This is hardly being a stickler for the truth when the Lord of Truth is being made to look as a liar. What the cessationism proponents do not realize (or maybe they do) is that their defense of their doctrine is denying the ministry of the Holy Spirit, thus denying the ministry of the Lord Jesus. His healing and miracle ministry were because He was anointed of the Holy Ghost. There is a clear parallel between the Upper Room of Acts for the disciples and the River Jordan and wilderness experience of Jesus. Both parties did not do any supernatural ministry until after being endued with power by the Holy Ghost.

> *And Jesus returned in the power of the Spirit into Galilee: and there went out a fame of Him through all the region round about* (Luke 4:14).

BEWARE OF CESSATIONISM

The Lord also warned us, "Take heed and beware of the leaven of the Pharisees and of the Sadducees....Then understood they how that He bade them not beware of the leaven of bread, but of the **doctrine of the Pharisees and of the Sadducees**"(Matt. 16:6,12). In the days of Jesus, the Pharisees and Sadducees were the two major religious groups. The Sadducees were those who did not believe much of anything supernatural. Cessationism and no supernatural powers were definitely part of the belief pattern of the Sadducees. Paul said, "A little leaven leaveneth the whole lump" (Gal. 5:9).

Today we have a lump of no supernatural power because of the leaven of *no* glossolalia and charismata. I want you to notice what Jesus said when questioned by Cessationist-Sadducees:

> *The same day came to Him **the Sadducees, which say that there is no resurrection**, and asked Him, Saying, Master, Moses said, If a man die, having no children, his brother shall marry his wife, and raise up seed unto his brother. Now there were with us seven brethren: and the first, when he had married a wife, deceased, and, having no issue, left his wife unto his brother: Likewise the second also, and the third, unto the seventh. And last of all the woman died also. Therefore in the resurrection whose wife shall she be of the seven? for they all had her. **Jesus answered and said unto them, Ye do err, not knowing the scriptures, nor the power of God** (Matthew 22:23-29).*

The Sadducees came with a supposedly very clever and exegetically difficult question to prove and justify their unbelieving doctrine. To better understand the reason behind the posing of their question, here is a little info in regard to the Sadducees. They were elitists who rigidly believed in maintaining the priestly order and caste, but were also liberal in their willingness to incorporate Hellenism into their lives. This was vehemently opposed by the Pharisees. They reckoned themselves to be Sola Scriptura and rejected the idea of the Oral Law, insisting on a literal interpretation of the Written Law, which is why they did not believe in the afterlife, since (according to their theology) it is not mentioned in the Torah. The primary focus of Sadducee life was rituals associated with the Temple. In effect, they were worshiping the intellectualism behind the Scripture without knowing the power of the Scripture.

Jesus answered them, "Ye do err, not knowing the scriptures, nor the power of God" (Matt. 22:29). That was a slap in the face of the Sadducees who prided themselves on being *Literalists* or *Sola Scriptura*, but Jesus told them, "You really don't know and are not acquainted with the Scripture." Thus, that is why there is no power...no *dunamis*, which simply means "ability and performance." In other words, the Lord was stating, *If you had known the Scripture like you claim you do, then you would have seen its performance and confirmation.* This is the exact spot of the Cessationist today who claims to be Bible believing but is only exuding mental assent and not mirroring living epistles. Mental assent is agreement to the fact that the Bible is true, but it is void of action and encompasses a subtle form of self-deception. Mental assent is the biggest enemy of faith and a robber of God's blessings in our lives. Cessationism claims Bible believing, but is not Bible acting. Cessationists would love for us to think and believe that Paul ended his lecture to the Corinthians concerning spiritual gifts with these words, "Wherefore, brethren, do not covet to prophesy, and forbid everyone to speak with tongues." This is *not* how he concluded.

> *But if anyone disregards or does not recognize [that it is a command of the Lord], he is disregarded and not recognized, [he is one whom God knows not]. So [to conclude], my brethren, earnestly desire and set your hearts on prophesying...and do not forbid or hinder speaking in [unknown] tongues* (1 Corinthians 14:38-39 AMP).

> *Wherefore, brethren, covet to prophesy, and forbid not to speak with tongues. Let all things be done decently and in order* (1 Corinthians 14:39-40).

> *...for this is God's will for you in Christ Jesus. Do not put out the Spirit's fire, do not treat prophecies with contempt* (1 Thessalonians 5:18-20 NIV).

> *But if any man be ignorant, let him be ignorant* (1 Corinthians 14:38).

ENDNOTE

1. Benjamin Warfield, *Counterfeit Miracles* 1918. Cornell University Library (July 8, 2009).

Chapter 4

BENEFITS OF PRAYING IN TONGUES (1-20)

Just as Paul was not ignorant to the power of prayer and speaking in tongues, neither were the early Christians. The early Christians understood that they could not neglect prayer.

> *But we will give ourselves continually to prayer and the ministry of the word* (Acts 6:4).

> *We shall be persevering to **the** prayer and **the** service of the saying (logos)* (Acts 6:4 New Testament Greek Interlinear).

They were a praying Church and how great and mighty things they achieved in prayer. Even when they became very busy in ministry, they did not allow business to get in the way of prayer. In the literal text it says, "We will persevere and give ourselves to the prayer...." Pay attention to the words *the prayer* not just *a prayer*. The word *the* is a definite article meaning "a determiner" that introduces a noun phrase and implies that the thing mentioned has already been mentioned and was common knowledge. The early Church comprehended that praying in tongues was *the* prayer. Praying in tongues was known as the prayer. The early Church gave much time and attention to it. This was common knowledge to the early disciples, and it should be so in the modern church.

Prayer, especially praying in tongues, is a vital aspect to spiritual growth and sensitivity in the spirit. There is no way around it! If you want to grow in the anointing, it is imperative that you become a person of prayer. Jesus was a Man of prayer, as was the apostle Paul, and the early Church was birthed and based on prayer. The Holy Writ (Bible) shows that prayer, and especially *tongues* played a very prominent role in the life of the early Church, and it must play a prominent role in your life.

The following are the first twenty of sixty benefits of praying in tongues. These benefits improve your life in many ways including your spiritual, emotional, physical, and relational well-being. The remaining forty benefits are described in the next two chapters.

1. *Tongues is the entrance into the supernatural.*

> *For he that speaketh in an unknown tongue speaketh not unto men, but unto God...howbeit in the spirit he speaketh mysteries* (1 Corinthians 14:2).

Praying in tongues is beneficial because it is the gateway into the spirit realm. There is a doorway into the realm of the spirit and it is through tongues. John said, "I was in the Spirit on the Lord's day" (Rev. 1:10). No wonder Christians have no knowledge of entering the spirit realm. Tongues are the key that unlock the spirit world. As long as satan can keep you away from tongues, he can keep you away from the miraculous. Notice the words, "howbeit in the spirit" (1 Cor. 14:2). When you pray in tongues, you are automatically in the spirit. Paul was stating that God is in the spirit, and when we pray in tongues we are in the spirit where God dwells. In other words, when you start praying in tongues you are entering God's *miracle zone.*

Tongues is the prayer in the New Testament.

2. *Praying in tongues is a direct line to God.*

First Corinthians 14:2 says, "For he that speaketh in an unknown tongue speaketh not unto men, but unto God...howbeit in the spirit he speaketh mysteries." Tongues is your hotline to God.

How many people would love to have an audience with God? Literally millions! There are people all over the world doing all kinds of crazy things to get their god to hear them. Some are piercing their bodies, and others are offering all kinds of sacrifices, but Paul reveals to us a direct line to the Almighty. People of all religions know that when we get an audience with God, miracles will flow.

Through tongues, you and I can have direct access to God. The Word says, "no one understandeth him…" (see 1 Cor. 14:2). This means satan does not understand when you pray in the spirit. He knows what you are doing, but he cannot understand what you are saying. He is helpless to sabotage your prayer. It is funny how people say, "Tongues is of the devil," and yet Paul says, "Tongues is talking to God." Through tongues, you have direct access to God.

Tongues is the believer's direct access to the throne room.

---

3. *Praying in tongues is speaking divine mysteries—divine coded secrets.*

Praying in tongues is speaking divine mysteries—divinely coded secrets. First Corinthians 14:2 says, "For he that speaketh in an unknown tongue speaketh not unto men, but unto God…howbeit in the spirit he speaketh mysteries." Notice the word *mysteries*. This is a loaded word that has multiple meanings, which are eye-opening. Some versions translate this word as "secrets." The Greek word is *musterion* and the meanings are:

- Hidden things
- Divine secrets
- Coded language
- Secret will or plan
- Secret counsels that govern God in His dealing with the righteous, hidden from the ungodly and wicked men but plain to the godly
- Knowledge withheld from ungodly, but truth revealed to the righteous

- Images and forms[1]

W.E. Vine's *Expository Dictionary of New Testament Words* defines mysteries as "primarily that which is known to the *mustes*, meaning they initiated from *mueo*, which means to initiate into the mysteries." In the New Testament, the word *mystery* does not denote "the mysterious," as with the English word. Rather, it denotes that which, being outside the range of unassisted natural apprehension, can be made known only by divine revelation, and is made known in a manner and at a time appointed by God to those who are illumined by His Spirit. In the ordinary sense, a "mystery" implies knowledge withheld; its Scriptural significance is truth revealed. Look at First Corinthians 14:2 again. It says, "no one understandeth him." This means satan does not understand what you are saying when you pray in the Spirit. Therefore, he cannot sabotage your prayer. Now look at this stated meaning, "But that which, being outside the range of unassisted natural apprehension, can be made known only by divine revelation." Therefore when you pray in tongues, secrets or plans will be made known to you. Let's look at some other translations of First Corinthians 14:2:

- The New International Version says, "For anyone who speaks in a tongue does not speak to men but to God. Indeed, no one understands him; he utters mysteries with his spirit."

- The Weymouth New Testament puts it this way, "Yet in the Spirit he is speaking secret truths."

- The Amplified Bible says, "...because in the [Holy] Spirit he utters secret truths and hidden things [not obvious to the understanding]."

When you pray in tongues, you are declaring the secrets of God, which will impart blessings and impact your life. You are prophesying your God-ordained future. By praying in the Spirit, you are making a path of blessings and power for you to walk in and enjoy.

Tongues is drawing secrets to life's complicated issues.

---

4. *Praying in tongues is prophesying your God-ordained future.*

Praying in tongues is prophesying and praying out God's plans for your life. Remember the word *musterion* from Point 3? It is defined as:

- Secret counsels that govern God in His dealing with the righteous, hidden from the ungodly and wicked men but plain to the godly.

- Knowledge withheld from ungodly, but truth revealed to the righteous.

- Secret will and plan.[2]

The anointing is strong when you are in the plan and will of God for your life. Many times people say, "I don't know what to do with my life!" or "I'm stuck!" or "I don't know where to begin!"

The plan is the wisdom of God, and it is hidden *for* the believer and not *from* the believer. When you discover the plan of God, then you have uncovered the wisdom of God. Paul says, "We speak the wisdom of God in a mystery" (1 Cor. 2:7). How? By praying or speaking in tongues. Solomon in his wisdom declared, "wisdom is profitable to direct" (Eccles. 10:10). The plan of God is divine direction for your life, ministry, job, or any area of your life. Your next step in life and ministry will be revealed to you as you pray in the Holy Ghost. Many times, even when we know the plan of God for our lives, we do not know how to implement or how to get it done. Again, that's why we must pray in the Holy Ghost to get the step-by-step plan that leads to the overall plan.

Tongues is entrance into the realm of the spirit—the miraculous zone.

---

5. *Praying in tongues is strengthening your inner self with might.*

Ephesians 3:16 tells us, "That He would grant you, according to the riches of His glory, to be strengthened with might by His Spirit in the inner man." The Weymouth New Testament words it like this,

"To grant you—in accordance with the wealth of His glorious perfections—to be strengthened by His Spirit with power penetrating to your inmost being." To *strengthen* means "to make stronger." It also means "to increase in strength and force." According to the apostle Paul, when you pray in tongues, you are strengthening or fortifying your spirit man with might. Obviously, he would know more about the might of tongues, as he declared to the Corinthian saints that he prayed in tongues more than them all (see 1 Cor. 14:18). The word *might* is the Greek word *dunamis*, and it means "miracle power and explosive power." The more you pray in the spirit, the more you are increasing in spiritual force on the inside of you. The more you pray in tongues, the more explosive power and miraculous power are growing inside of you. How can you be depressed when the strength of God is within you? Just like barbells will build up your arms, praying in tongues will build up your spirit. When your spirit is strong, it will help to keep that flesh body of yours in line.

The more you pray in the spirit, the more you are increasing in spiritual force within.

Praying in tongues keeps you spiritually fit.

---

6. *Praying in tongues is praying things that have been concealed to be revealed.*

   ...they spoke with tongues and prophesied (Acts 19:6).

   Praying in tongues is prophetic in its nature. Jesus utters these wonderful words in the Gospel, "...out of his belly shall flow rivers of living water" (John 7:38). The Greek word for *flow* is *rheo*.[3] It means "to flow, stream, utter, say or speak." The English term *rhetoric* meaning "elaborate eloquence," finds its root from this Greek word. Another similar and Charismatic-Pentecostal understood word, *rhema*, comes from this root word, rheo. Therefore, when you are praying in tongues, you are declaring the rhemas of God. You are decreeing and prophesying your future.

Tongues pulls you from the past into the future.

---

7. *Praying in tongues is home improvement and a source of spiritual edification.*

He that speaketh in an unknown tongue edifieth himself... (1 Corinthians 14:4).

...edifies and improves himself... (1 Corinthians 14:4 AMP).

...he who speaks in an unknown tongue does good to himself... (Weymouth New Testament 1 Corinthians 14:4).

...those who speak in strange tongues help only themselves... (1 Corinthians 14:4 GNB).

Paul was encouraging the Corinthian church to keep praying and worshiping in tongues as a means of spiritual edification. Other versions of the Bible use the words *improves*, *does good*, *builds*, and *help themselves* to define "edification." How many of us could use some improvements right now? Tongues will improve and build you up in a down world. In fact, we can safely say that tongues is "doing home improvement." The word *edify* is the Greek word *oikodomeo*, which is a compound of two words: *oiko* meaning "house" and *domeo* meaning "to build."[4] When you put these two words together, it means "to build a house." This word *edify* also means "to charge up like you would charge a dead battery." This verse could be literally translated as, "He who speaks or prays in unknown tongues builds his house and charges himself up with a spiritual current."

Have you ever felt drained and physically worn out? I have! Because I travel extensively to minister worldwide, many times I cross time zones and spend long hours in planes and airports. When I get to my destination, I am often physically drained. But I thank God for the ability to charge my body with spiritual energy through the avenue of tongues. This simple habit of praying in tongues has helped me again and again.

**Tongues is building a strong premise
to carry the anointing.**

---

8. *Praying in tongues builds and stimulates your faith.*

> *But ye, beloved, building up yourselves on your most holy faith, praying in the Holy Ghost* (Jude 1:20).

> *But you, beloved, build yourselves up [founded] on your most holy faith [make progress, rise like an edifice higher and higher], praying in the Holy Spirit* (Jude 1:20 AMP).

In this tiny epistle, Jude warns of a time of great apostasy in the last days where right would be considered wrong and vice versa. These will be tough times! You do not need to be a rocket scientist to realize that we are living in these days of apostasy. What we need in these tough times is strong and stimulated faith. Jude tells us that when we pray in the Holy Ghost, we are building and stimulating our world with overcoming faith. Praying in tongues is a faith booster. As you pray in tongues, you will rise higher and higher in a "down" world. The Amplified Bible aptly translates this verse, "Build yourselves up [founded] on your most holy faith [make progress, rise like an edifice higher and higher], praying in the Holy Spirit" (Jude 1:20). Notice it says "make progress." The world system under satan's influence is designed to hinder your progress in every sense of the word, but as you keep praying in tongues, your progress will become unstoppable and undeniable by your worst enemies.

Praying in tongues makes your progress unstoppable and undeniable before your enemies.

---

9. *Praying in tongues is giving praise and thanksgiving well unto God.*

> *What is it then? I will pray with the spirit, and I will pray with the understanding also: I will sing with the spirit, and I will sing with the understanding also. Else when thou shalt bless with the spirit, how shall he that occupieth the room of the unlearned say Amen at thy giving of thanks, seeing he understandeth not what thou sayest? For thou verily givest thanks well...* (1 Corinthians 14:15-17).

Praying in tongues is good for you because it is another way of praising and blessing the Lord. When you release tongues you are releasing praise and thanksgiving to God. Did you notice Paul says, "For thou verily giveth thanks well," meaning this is bonafide praise. It is singing with grace in your heart.

> *Let the word of Christ dwell in you richly in all wisdom; teaching and admonishing one another in psalms and hymns and spiritual songs, singing with grace in your hearts to the Lord* (Colossians 3:16).

Spiritual songs is not a reference to gospel music, although that is included. The term *spiritual songs* refers to songs from your spirit, the tongues of praise and thanksgiving that flow from your heart and through your mouth. I guarantee you that there is not one ounce of unbelief in tongues. When you are speaking or singing in tongues, there is no fear, doubt, unbelief, panic, or depression attached to it.

There is not one ounce of unbelief in praying in tongues.

---

10. *Praying in tongues is praying in line with the divine will of God.*

> *Likewise the Spirit also helpeth our infirmities: for we know not what we should pray for as we ought: but the Spirit itself maketh intercession for us with groanings which cannot be uttered. And He that searcheth the hearts knoweth what is the mind of the Spirit, because He maketh intercession for the saints according to the will of God. And we know that all things work together for good to them that love God, to them who are the called according to His purpose* (Romans 8:26-28).

In the eighth chapter of his Roman epistle, Paul gave us a very important insight into praying in tongues and its function in the spirit world. The Holy Spirit is our Helper, Intercessor, and Comforter. He is here to help us in every area of our lives and particularly in prayer. Effective prayer has to be done according to the will of God and by faith. God does not answer and listen to unbelief. Always remember that prayer does not change God. It changes things, and it changes you. God is unchangeable. He answers our prayers, which are anchored in faith and according to His divine word. Malachi 3:6 says, "For I am the Lord, I change not." As our Helper, the Holy Spirit helps us to pray. The Greek word Paul used is *sunantilam-banomai*, and it means "taking hold together, with, and against."[5] Of course this verse is referring to tongues because Paul says, "the Spirit itself maketh intercession for us with groanings which cannot be uttered" (Rom. 8:26). *Groanings* in the Bible does not mean moaning or complaining. It always alludes to prayer and intercession.

You can see this fact revealed in the Hebrew people in their moment of distress, and Jesus at the grave of Lazarus. (See Exodus 2:23-25 and John 11:33,38.) The word *groaning* here can also be translated as "that which cannot be uttered in articulate speech." Articulate speech would be English or your natural mother tongue. So we understand that "groaning" is talking about praying in tongues. Many times we do not know exactly how we are to approach a situation in prayer, but thank God the Holy Spirit inside us comes to our aid as we pray in tongues. He comes against the problem and holds us together. Side by side, we stand against the enemy to remove him. There is no hope for the devil! When you do not know what to say in prayer, the Holy Spirit knows exactly what to say, and it is always in line with God's will. You cannot fail with the Holy Spirit involved in your prayer life.

Tongues is speaking the language and will of God.

---

11. *Praying in tongues is help with our ultimate weakness—lack of knowledge.*

What is the believer's ultimate weakness? The prophet Hosea in his writing revealed God's heartache, "My people are destroyed for a lack of knowledge" (Hosea 4:6). Knowledge does not just imply information but also the know-how. Not knowing and not knowing how is the ultimate destruction of God's people. Now look at the apostle Paul's dilemma and solution:

68

Likewise the Spirit also helpeth our infirmities: for we know not what we should pray for as we ought: but the Spirit itself maketh intercession for us with groanings which cannot be uttered (Romans 8:26).

When Paul uses the word *help*, he is painting a picture of assistance afforded to infants not able to support themselves, or to the feeble, staggering and barely able to walk. It means to relieve those whose strength is insufficient to carry their burden alone. The word *infirmities* in Greek is *astheneia* meaning, "weakness, shortcoming, lack of strength and incapacity."[6] This word is not referring to physical disease but much more to our limitations or deficiencies. The weakness spoken here is that of the believer's inability and inefficiency of how to properly and accurately engage a situation in prayer. We understand the generality of prayer but how to specifically engage which types of prayer for a given situation is beyond the grasp of the believer. Our ultimate weakness, therefore, is not knowing how to properly pray. This is where in praying in tongues, the Holy Spirit gives assistance in that He knows exactly how to pray about the situation.

Tongues is the ultimate assistance in prayer.

---

12. Praying in tongues enables all things to work for your good.

…because He maketh intercession for the saints according to the will of God. And we know that all things work together for good to them that love God, to them who are the called according to His purpose (Romans 8:27-28).

"All things work together for good" is an expression that many Christians have used to put a nice face on a bad situation. Some have used it in death, accidents, and other disappointing situations. This verse was not given by the inspiration of the Holy Spirit to excuse failures. This verse belongs to the tongue-talker. It is when you pray in tongues that all things will work for your good. Notice it says something is working for your good. Praying and interceding in tongues is working on your behalf to bring good to your life.

13. *Praying in tongues aids us in being God-inside minded.*

> *Even the Spirit of truth; whom the world cannot receive, because it seeth Him not, neither knoweth Him: but ye know Him; for He dwelleth with you, and shall be in you* (John 14:17).

Praying in tongues will be of great benefit to you because it is a constant reminder of the presence and power of the indwelling Holy Spirit. Continuous praying and worshiping in tongues will help you to be consciously aware of the reality of the indwelling Spirit. This realization will cause you to rely more on His ability rather than yours. His power is more effective than all human abilities and talents. This is the word of the Lord unto Zerubbabel, saying, "Not by might, nor by power, but by My Spirit, saith the Lord of hosts" (Zech. 4:6). "For ye have not received the spirit of bondage again to fear; but ye have received the Spirit of adoption, whereby we cry, Abba, Father. The Spirit itself beareth witness with our spirit, that we are the children of God: And if children, then heirs; heirs of God, and joint-heirs with Christ..." (Rom. 8:15-17). As you keep praying in tongues, it enables you to be consciously aware of the fact that you are a child of God, a joint heir with Jesus, and that the Holy Spirit indwells you.

Tongues renders the believer to be God-minded and miracle-minded.

---

14. *Praying in tongues magnifies God.*

> *"And they of the circumcision which believed were astonished, as many as came with Peter, because that on the Gentiles also was poured out the gift of the Holy Ghost. For they heard them speak with tongues, and magnify God"* (Acts 10:45-46).

Apart from meaning "praise and thanksgiving to God," *magnify* means "to increase in size and capacity." When you are praying in tongues, God is getting bigger and bigger on the inside of you. The bigger God gets inside of you, the smaller the devil will be.

Tongues enlarges your perception of God's power in your life.

---

15. Praying in tongues gives spiritual refreshing and rest.

Praying in tongues is good for you because it refreshes and gives spiritual rest.

> *For with stammering lips and another tongue will he speak to this people. To whom he said, This is the rest wherewith ye may cause the weary to rest; and this is the refreshing...* (Isaiah 28:11-12).

Tongues will give you rest in the midst of warfare. We all know that we are in a fight, and if we are not cautious we can get battle-weary. Thank God we can always get refreshed and rested as we release our prayer language. Peter, in the Book of Acts terms it as, "...times of refreshing...from the presence of the Lord"(Acts 3:19).

This is how Paul kept himself strong, refreshed, and on the cutting edge, even though all hell was assigned against him. The man constantly prayed in tongues and thanked God that he spoke more in tongues than the Corinthian church.

Tongues increases your sharpness and accuracy in the anointing.

---

16. Praying in tongues helps you to enter the world of the gifts of the Spirit.

The nine gifts of the Spirit are for us today. They give the believer the supernatural edge that we need to operate in the world. The nine fruits of the Spirit are for us to reflect the character of Jesus, but the gifts of the Spirit are for us to manifest the power of Jesus. As we tap into the power of praying in tongues, it will open us up to the gifts. It will be far easier to move in the vocal gifts, the power gifts, and revelatory gifts of the Spirit as we open up our lives to the catalyst of tongues. Our heavenly language of tongues is the gift that unlocks all the other gifts.

You will notice those who do not believe in the baptism of Holy Spirit with the evidence of tongues also do not believe in healing, miracles, and casting out of devils. Apparently—according to doubters—it is all passed away. The moment you shut down tongues, you shut down the miraculous nine gifts from your life. The majority of ministers who have had great healing ministries such as Oral Roberts, John G. Lake, or Smith Wigglesworth affirms that speaking in tongues was a very important key to their ministry. Here is the secret of success of John G. Lake in his own words, "I want to talk with the utmost frankness, and say to you, that **TONGUES HAVE BEEN THE MAKING OF MY MINISTRY.** It is that peculiar communication with God when God reveals to my soul the truth I utter to you day by day in the ministry. Many times I climb out of bed, take my pencil and pad, and jot down the beautiful things of God, the wonderful things of God that He talks out in my spirit and reveals to my heart."[7]

Tongues enables the believer access to the wonders of God.

---

17. Praying in tongues is fine-tuning your spirit man to be sensitive and hear the voice of God.

The more we pray in tongues, the more our spirit becomes sensitive to the Holy Spirit. We adjust our spiritual tuner by praying in other tongues. Pay attention to the ideas, concepts, and insights that flow to your mind from your spirit as you pray in tongues. This is God giving you keys for your victory. Through tongues, God communicates to you the steps to take to secure your victory on the earth. Tongues is not just you talking to God, but it's Him talking to you, giving you insights and keys to your problems. Many people just blast in tongues like bullets from a machine gun and then jump up and go. Take time to listen to what the Holy Spirit is saying. That is what happened to John on the Isle of Patmos where he was sent to suffer and die by his enemies. Satan could not have anticipated what happened next. "For with stammering lips and another tongue will he speak to this people" (Isa. 28:11). Now let's read John's account:

> *I was in the Spirit* on the Lord's day, and heard behind me a great voice, as of a trumpet, Saying, I am Alpha and Omega, the First and the Last: and, what thou seest, write in a book, and send it unto the seven churches which are in Asia; unto Ephesus, and unto Smyrna, and unto Pergamos, and unto Thyatira, and unto Sardis, and unto Philadelphia, and unto Laodicea. And I turned to see the voice that spake with me (Revelation 1:10-12).

John was not on vacation in Patmos. He had some serious trouble and needed God to deliver him. Notice what he said, *"I was in the Spirit."* The apostle Paul has already told us that when we pray in tongues we are in the Spirit. (See First Corinthians 14:2.) John accessed the realm of the Spirit by praying in tongues, and when he did, he heard the voice of the Lord.

You will hear the voice of the Lord when you are in the Spirit. John said he heard His voice as a trumpet and Paul said that the trumpet prepares you for war and gets you ready to fight your enemies. One word from God will change your entire life. A word from God is worth more than ten thousand words from humankind. God knows something about your problem that no one else knows. He knows how to deliver you, and as you pray in tongues, He drops the answer into your spirit and the rest is victory.

> In the law it is written, With men of other tongues and other lips will I speak unto this people; and yet for all that will they not hear Me, saith the Lord (1 Corinthians 14:21).

18. Praying in tongues assists you in bringing your natural tongue under control.

Praying in tongues will be beneficial to you in your endeavor to control your tongue.

The Book of Proverbs tells us that death and life are in the power of the tongue. (See Proverbs 18:21.) Control your tongue and you will control your life. Praying in tongues will keep you from profane, vulgar, and obscene communication. When you develop the habit of praying in tongues, you will not have time to gossip about other people, tell dirty jokes, or be involved with any other filthy communication.

19. *Praying in tongues helps you to develop intimacy with the Holy Spirit.*

Praying in tongues is God's method of bypassing the human mind in prayer and allowing spirit to Spirit communion with God. Tongues is the language inspired by the Holy Spirit. There is something amazing about speaking and understanding the same language. It creates affinity and connectivity. Imagine finding yourself in a foreign land that does not speak your mother tongue. You look and feel like a stranger, and all of a sudden you hear somebody speaking your language. Your ears perk up, and all of a sudden that person is like your long lost relative. Language connects people. Tongues will connect you to God. Through the avenue of praying in tongues, we can know God for ourselves in a personal and intimate way by His Spirit working from the inside of us. The Message Bible beautifully pens First Corinthians 14:2, "If you praise Him in the private language of tongues, God understands you but no one else does, for you are sharing intimacies just between you and Him." The eighteenth verse of the same translation caps what praying in tongues is all about, *"I'm grateful to God for the gift of praying in tongues that He gives us for praising Him, which leads to wonderful intimacies we enjoy with Him. I enter into this as much or more than any of you."*

20. *Praying in tongues creates an air of privacy between you and God.*

Those of us who have been blessed to be fluent in two or more languages find we can use that for exclusivity and privacy. Although I speak fluent English, my mother-tongue is Creole and French. Those are the languages I spoke until my family moved to London. Even though I left Mauritius many years ago, I can still converse in French and Creole. That comes in handy when I want to say something to my brothers that I don't want others around us to understand. When you are praying in tongues—your heavenly language— you completely cut satan off. He would love to know what you are saying, but he doesn't have a clue. It is a private conversation between you and your heavenly Father.

ENDNOTES

1. W.E. Vine, *Vines Expository of Greek New Testament Words* #3466 (Nashville, TN: Thomas Nelson).

2. Ibid.

3. Strong's Concordance #G4482, s.v. *flow*.

4. Ibid. #G3618.

5. Ibid. #G4878.

6. Ibid. #G769.

7. http://www.tentmaker.org/holy-spirit/baptism1.htm; accessed April 06, 2010.

Chapter 5

BENEFITS OF PRAYING IN TONGUES (21-40)

We are delving into how powerful and beneficial tongues are for us today. The Word of God is loaded with revelations to bless your life and take you to the next level. Everything that you are reading is for you to experience victory in Christ Jesus over the world, the flesh, and the devil. Let us further look in the benefits of praying in other tongues.

21. Praying in tongues will deepen your relationship with God.

It is difficult to deepen your relationship with someone if both of you speak different languages. The lack of understanding becomes a major barrier to a deep, meaningful relationship, even if you have a lot of other things in common. Speaking God's language will enable you to deepen your relationship and fellowship with Him. Never forget how *deep* you go with God will determine how high you will go in life. Think about these Scriptures:

> *Acquaint now thyself with Him, and be at peace: thereby good shall come unto thee* (Job 22:21).

> *Deep calleth unto deep...* (Psalm 42:7).

They that go down to the sea in ships, that do business in great waters; These see the works of the Lord, and His wonders in the deep (Psalm 107:23-24).

Tongues is deep calling unto deep.

---

22. *Praying in tongues will give you access to revelation knowledge.*

Praying in tongues causes your spirit to tap the mind of God and to receive understanding from His Word. Many believers complain that they fall asleep when they read the Bible. That is because they are not able to access the hidden treasures of the Scriptures.

But we speak the wisdom of God in a mystery, even the hidden wisdom, which God ordained before the world unto our glory: Which none of the princes of this world knew: for had they known it, they would not have crucified the Lord of glory. But as it is written, Eye hath not seen, nor ear heard, neither have entered into the heart of man, the things which God hath prepared for them that love Him. But God hath revealed them unto us by His Spirit: for the Spirit searcheth all things, yea, the deep things of God. For what man knoweth the things of a man, save the spirit of man which is in him? even so the things of God knoweth no man, but the Spirit of God. Now we have received, not the spirit of the world, but the spirit which is of God; that we might know the things that are freely given to us of God (1 Corinthians 2:7-12).

Now look at Romans 8:7, "Because the carnal mind is enmity against God: for it is not subject to the law of God, neither indeed can be." Then First Corinthians 2:14, "But the natural man receiveth not the things of the Spirit of God: for they are foolishness unto him: neither can he know them, because they are spiritually discerned."

Praying in tongues will open the Bible to you from God's perspective and not just from an intellectual level. Many theologians know the Bible from an intellectual level, and there is no power in their lives. There are great truths that are yet to be revealed, and you can access them through tongues.

23. Praying in tongues is part of the offensive of the armor of God. It is the lance that will shoot down the enemy.

> *Wherefore take unto you the whole armour of God, that ye may be able to withstand in the evil day, and having done all, to stand. Stand therefore, having your loins girt about with truth, and having on the breastplate of right-eousness; And your feet shod with the preparation of the gospel of peace; Above all, taking the shield of faith, wherewith ye shall be able to quench all the fiery darts of the wicked. And take the helmet of salvation, and the sword of the Spirit, which is the word of God: Praying al-ways with all prayer and supplication in the Spirit, and watching thereunto with all perseverance and supplication for all saints* (Ephesians 6:13-18).

"The whole armor of God": Pay attention to the words *whole armor*. *Whole armor* refers to the Greek word *panoplia*, meaning "whole, complete set." It was a word used to depict the full armor of a hoplite or heavily-armed Roman soldier. Whenever the Roman soldier would put on his full armor, there were seven things that he would put on. The apostle Paul listed all the other Roman weapon-ries by name except for the lance. No Roman panoply would be complete without the lance. Since *six* is "the number of man" and *seven* is "the number of God," seven stands for completion. That is why in the Old Testament we see and read of the seven feasts of Is-rael, seven sacrifices, seven furnitures of the tabernacle, seven lamps of the candlestick, seven pillars of wisdom, and seven cities of refuge to name a few. The New Testament, specifically the Book of Revela-tion talks of the seven churches, Seven Spirits of God, seven golden candlesticks, seven stars, seven lamps of fire, seven seals, seven horns and seven trumpets to name a few.

God does things in sevens, and the seventh weaponry of the armor of God is the lance of prayer in the spirit. The Roman lance was called a pilum. It was the typical legionary weapon together with the short sword gladius. It was designed to penetrate the shield as well as the soldier holding it, and to bend upon impact to make it unusable for another opponent. The pilum was used for long distances by throwing it, and for shorter distances they would use it to charge. It was a very offensive weapon. Praying in tongues is an aggressive and offensive weapon to put holes in the cover of the devil. The lance of tongues is designed to paralyze the movements of the devil against your life. No wonder the devil fights tongues so much, as it causes great harm in his kingdom.

Tongues is the lance to throw and cause great damage in the kingdom of darkness.

---

24. *Praying in tongues helps us to do what Jesus said to do in the Garden of Gethsemane...pray for at least one hour.*

> *And He cometh unto the disciples, and findeth them asleep, and saith unto Peter, What, could ye not watch with Me one hour?* (Matthew 26:40)

Tongues enable us to pray much. Paul commands the Church, "Pray without ceasing" (1 Thess. 5:17). While it is true there are many kinds of prayer, it is the ability to pray in tongues at any time, without running out of words or vocabulary, that permits you to stay in prayer for a long stretch of time. There are believers today who struggle to pray more than five minutes, as they do not know what to say to the Lord. Tongues are the avenue whereby we can communicate well with God. While speaking in tongues, the mind is not taxed and can focus while the spirit prays. This great privilege of praying in tongues helps us to pray about a difficult situation when we do not even know how to approach it in prayer in our known language.

Tongues enables us to pray through.

---

25. *Praying in tongues helps synchronize us with the timing of God.*

> *Whereupon Jesus said to them, My time (opportunity) has not come yet; but any time is suitable for you and your opportunity is ready any time [is always here]* (John 7:6 AMP).

God's plans for our lives, are *timing-dependent*. In the Bible and in the Greek language, there are two words for time. They are *chronos* and *kairos*. Obviously, from *chronos* we get our English words *chronology* and *chronological*, which relate to the establishment of dates and time sequences. *Chronos* is measured in terms of seconds, minutes, hours, days, weeks, months, and years. *Kairos*, on the other hand, is an ancient Greek word meaning "the right or opportune moment," or better still, "the supreme moment." While *chronos* refers to chronological or sequential time, the latter (kairos) signifies a time in between, a moment of undetermined period of time in which something special happens. While *chronos* is quantitative, *kairos* has a qualitative nature. In the Bible, *kairos* is to describe the qualitative form of time. It is "a passing instant when an opening appears which must be driven through with force if success is to be achieved." Furthermore, in the New Testament, *kairos* means "the appointed time in the purpose of God," the time when God acts.

Time has to do with chronological time, while *timing* is the accomplishment of series of events to create an opportune time to act. To avoid frustration in life, the believer must understand time and timing. The supernatural is timing-based. In a situation, all the external may be presently pointing for success, and yet, if the timing is wrong, failure and disappointment will ensue. It can be very costly to do what looks like a godly thing or good idea at the wrong time. Millions of believers and ministers do it on a daily basis. There must be a synchronization so that we do not step before the right time and hurt ourselves. Most mistakes in executing the plans of God, especially in ministries, come from a poor understanding of God's timing. Regardless of how much planning, sensitivity to God's timing is more important. Many times, the timing of God will not synchronize with your natural thinking.

> *Now when they had gone throughout Phrygia and the region of Galatia, and were forbidden of the Holy Ghost to preach the word in Asia, After they were come to Mysia, they assayed to go into Bithynia: but the Spirit suffered them not. And they passing by Mysia came down to Troas. And a vision appeared to Paul in the night; There stood a man of Macedonia, and prayed him, saying, Come over*

into Macedonia, and help us. And after he had seen the vision, immediately we endeavoured to go into Macedonia, assuredly gathering that the Lord had called us for to preach the gospel unto them (Acts 16:6-10).

"...forbidden of the Holy Ghost to preach the word in Asia...but the Spirit suffered them not" (Acts 16:6-7). Someone once said, "I can go everywhere because God said to go into all the world to preach the Gospel." That is a true statement, but it is to the entire Church or Body of Christ, not just to an individual. In order to be fruitful, a believer or minister must know where God has sent him or her and His timing. The Great Commission applied to Paul too; so why did the Holy Spirit stop him from going to Asia? Paul was to go where the Holy Spirit guided him to go. There must be a synchronization between the plan and the timing of God's plan for our lives to experience great breakthroughs. Most synchronization will bring about an adjustment in plan. This is where praying in tongues plays an all important role. It will keep you sensitive and flexible to those adjustments. As you pray in tongues, there is an alignment that takes place in your spirit to God's timing. A synchronization occurs, an adjustment to God's plans that helps you embrace what looks like God's detours, but in reality God is maneuvering you into His kairos moment for your life. When we synchronize with God's timing, we come into prepared places and prepared people. I really like The Message translation of this event.

They went to Phrygia, and then on through the region of Galatia. Their plan was to turn west into Asia province, but the Holy Spirit blocked that route. So they went to Mysia and tried to go north to Bithynia, but the Spirit of Jesus wouldn't let them go there either. Proceeding on through Mysia, they went down to the seaport Troas. That night Paul had a dream: A Macedonian stood on the far shore and called across the sea, "Come over to Macedonia and help us!" The dream gave Paul his map. We went to work at once getting things ready to cross over to Macedonia. All the pieces had come together. We knew now for sure that God had called us to preach the good news to the Europeans (Acts 16:6-10 TM).

Notice they had a plan, and though noble, it was not God's plan for them at that time. If they'd refused to synchronize their lives with the Spirit, they would have been flustered, but when they were commissioned to the Macedonian's call, the Scripture states, *"All the pieces...came together."* As you pray in tongues and align yourself with the plan and timing of God, you too will be able to say, "All the pieces came together."

Tongues is alignment with the timing of God.

---

26. *Praying in tongues gives a door of utterance, boldness in preaching and teaching.*

The apostle Peter was transformed from a weak and insipid believer to a great and powerful preacher after he spoke in tongues. This is the same man who, a few days prior, had denied the Lord three times because of his fear of death. (See Matthew 26:69-75.) After speaking in tongues, however, he was able to boldly and fluently proclaim the Gospel of Jesus Christ. Peter, full of the Holy Spirit, preached a powerful message that brought conviction to the thousands under the sound of his voice.

> *This is that which was spoken by the prophet Joel: "And it shall come to pass in the last days, saith God, I will pour out My Spirit upon all flesh: and your sons and your daughters shall prophesy, and your young men shall see visions, and your old men shall dream dreams: and on My servants and on My handmaidens I will pour out in those days of My Spirit; and they shall prophesy: and I will shew wonders in heaven above, and signs in the earth beneath..."* (Acts 2:16-19).

Peter then further declared that Jesus Christ who had been crucified and raised from the dead, was their long-awaited Messiah and Lord! (See Acts 2:32-33,36.) This is an about turn from the man who vehemently swore and called curses upon himself saying, "I don't know the man"(see Matt. 26:74). Notice the transformation after tongues.

And when they had prayed, the place was shaken where they were assembled together; and they were all filled with the Holy Ghost, and they spake the word of God with boldness (Acts 4:31).

Tongues is for effective service.

---

27. *Tongues sows to the spirit.*

For he that soweth to his flesh shall of the flesh reap corruption; but he that soweth to the Spirit shall of the Spirit reap life everlasting (Galatians 6:8).

For whatever a man is in the habit of sowing, this also will he reap; because the one who sows with a view to his own evil nature, from his evil nature as a source shall reap corruption. But the one who sows with a view to the Spirit, from the Spirit as a source shall reap eternal life eternal (Galatians 6:8-10 Kenneth Wuest Expanded Translation).

He that sows to the spirit shall out of the deposit of the spirit reap the super abundant life. When you are praying in tongues, you are sowing in and to the spirit. According to Paul, when we pray in tongues, our spirit man is praying and speaking mysteries in the spirit (see 1 Cor. 14:2). Praying in tongues is making heavenly deposits, and out of those deposits you are gathering great interest for a better future. There is great return from your deposit of praying in tongues. Praying in the spirit and sowing in the spirit are not wasted time. Praying in tongues is investing in yourself for better returns. What you put in "tongues stocks" will pay good dividends in the short and long haul.

28. *Tongues is pulling out treasure in earthen vessels.*

Paul in his epistle to the Corinthians states, "We have this treasure in earthen vessels" (2 Cor. 4:7). The anointing and the glory are the treasures inside of us. However, what is the point of having treasure that is locked and you cannot get to it. Through tongues, we pull on the treasure that is resident inside of us. Your spirit is the chamber that holds the treasures of God. There is treasure in you and tongues is the avenue to drill the treasure oil out of you.

29. *Praying in tongues is not leaning upon your own understanding.*

> *Trust in the Lord with all thine heart; and lean not unto thine own understanding* (Proverbs 3:5).

> *For if I pray in an unknown tongue, my spirit prayeth, but my understanding is unfruitful* (1 Corinthians 14:14).

Leaning upon our own understanding leads to leaning upon our flesh, which God has warned against.

> *Thus saith the Lord; Cursed be the man that trusteth in man, and maketh flesh his arm, and whose heart departeth from the Lord. For he shall be like the heath in the desert, and shall not see when good cometh; but shall inhabit the parched places in the wilderness, in a salt land and not inhabited. Blessed is the man that trusteth in the Lord, and whose hope the Lord is. For he shall be as a tree planted by the waters, and that spreadeth out her roots by the river, and shall not see when heat cometh, but her leaf shall be green; and shall not be careful in the year of drought, neither shall cease from yielding fruit* (Jeremiah 17:5-8).

When we pray in tongues, we are clearly not leaning upon our understanding, as Paul states. Many times, our understanding of a situation will tell us that it is beyond our reach and hopelessness sets in. Our understanding is shaped by our education, environment, and experience; and based upon those things, we come to conclusions about life's circumstances. One thing is for sure, it does not matter how much we think we know, our understanding is limited compared to God. However, when we pray in tongues, we are not consulting with the conclusion of our understanding but leaning upon the understanding and ways of God which are higher than ours.

Tongues is the Holy Spirit searching your heart and praying through you the perfect will of God.

---

30. *Praying in tongues is blowing the ram's horn.*

In the Old Testament, the ram's horn or shofar was blown to call an assembly to war, to call an assembly to worship, to stir panic in the camp of the enemy and to announce a victory. When Joshua and Israel came to Jericho, at the long blast of the ram's horn, they shouted and the walls fell down flat and they took the city for God. Tongues is the blast that will bring down the walls that satan has erected in our lives to block us. Just as the people surrounded the walls of Jericho then shouted on the seventh day, we must learn to encircle our situations with tongues to bring the wall down.

Tongues is the rallying sound of victory.

31. *Praying in tongues is the releasing of angels*

When you pray in tongues, you are also releasing angels on assignment of deliverance. The Church prayed without ceasing for Peter when he was under a death sentence, and an angel was assigned to release and deliver him. (See Acts 12:4-10.) Let's look at Peter's testimony of his own deliverance from the hand of an evil king who had evil intent against him, "...Now I know of a surety, that the Lord hath sent His angel, and hath delivered me out of the hand of Herod, and from all the expectation of the people of the Jews" (Acts 12:11). When Rhoda went to see who was knocking at the door in the night and recognized Peter's voice, she ran back in the house where the company of believers were praying saying, "Peter is at the door" (see Acts 12:13-14). The people who had gathered thought she was mad but when she insisted, the church said, "It is his angel"(Acts 12:15).

Now let's connect this with Paul's words to the Corinthians, "Though I speak with the tongues of men and of angels..."(1 Cor. 13:1). You see, there are *tongues of men* and there are *tongues of angels*. Communications provoke movement and actions. When we pray in tongues, we are releasing angels on assignment of deliverance. Angels are agents of help and deliverance assigned by God for you, an heir of salvation. (See Hebrews 2.)

Tongues is releasing angels on heavenly assignments to change earthly situations.

---

32. Praying in tongues is a brainstorming session with God.

Brainstorm means, "To try to solve a problem by thinking intensely about it." The clear and often sudden understanding of a complex situation. The Holy Spirit is our problem solver. Our God-Assigned Helper. When we pray in other tongues, He interfaces our spirit with the limitless possibilities in the mind of God.

> *But, on the contrary, as the Scripture says, What eye has not seen and ear has not heard and has not entered into the heart of man, [all that] God has prepared (made and keeps ready) for those who love Him [who hold Him in affectionate reverence, promptly obeying Him and gratefully recognizing the benefits He has bestowed]. Yet to us God has unveiled and revealed them by and through His Spirit, for the [Holy] Spirit searches diligently, exploring and examining everything, even sounding the profound and bottomless things of God [the divine counsels and things hidden and beyond man's scrutiny]* (1 Corinthians 2:9-10 AMP).

When we pray in tongues, the Holy Spirit begins to probe into the "bottomless things of God"—His divine counsel concerning you, your ministry, relationships, business, and future. The search is beyond the bandwidth of humanity's scrutiny. It takes the help of the Holy Spirit to reach this depth of pre-arranged knowledge. Praise God, it has been hidden away for you and needs to be discovered by you in the spirit. That implies getting answers beyond your education, qualifications, and experiences in life. Answers evolve directly from the throne of God...answers that no force of hell can annul!

Tongues accesses the mind of God.

---

33. *Praying in tongues is entry into the creative highway.*

Creativity and innovation are what drive the 21st century. In any aspect of life where you are not innovative, you will become irrelevant. The story of George Washington Carver creating 105 recipes that included peanuts and over 100 other uses for peanuts, including paints, bio-fuel, and bio-plastic by fellowshipping with the Spirit of God, serves as a great example. What people can achieve in life beyond their ability, simply by knowing how to tap into the mind of the Spirit of God, is a feat that all believers must aspire to. This in itself will give you a creative life.

To create is the Hebrew word *bara*[1] meaning "to bring into existence that which never existed before." Praying in tongues gets you into the realms of creativity. Just like Adam before the Fall in the Garden of Eden, naming all the animals.

34. *Praying in tongues will overrule and overturn the death sentence and death assignment of the enemy against your life.*

To *overrule* means to "cancel, reverse, rescind, repeal, revoke, retract, disallow, override, veto, quash, overturn, overthrow, annul, nullify, invalidate, negate and make void" (New Oxford American Dictionary). This is exactly what the early Church did when Peter's life was under a death sentence. There was an evil assignment to take away his life. Herod had already brutally and unexpectantly beheaded James, and now he purposed to kill Peter. There were a few Herods mentioned in the Bible! Herod the Great, Herod Antipas (The Tetrarch), and Herod Agrippa. All three were evil and were bent on violence. You will remember when Salome asked for the head of John the Baptist on a platter, Herod the Tetrarch reluctantly agreed because of his oath. They did not like to be seen as changing their words. This would have been seen as a sign of weakness.

Now imagine yourself in Peter's shoes. You know that Herod, who had already murdered by decapitation your colleague John, has now approved and signed your death warrant. You know there is a death penalty and assignment against your life. What would you have done? What would you and your family have felt? I am sure, for many people, a sense of hopelessness would have surfaced.

> *And when he* [Herod] *had apprehended him, he put him in prison, and delivered him to four quaternions of soldiers to keep him; intending after Easter to bring him forth to the people. Peter therefore was kept in prison:* **but prayer was made without ceasing of the church unto God for him.** *And when Herod would have brought him forth, the same night Peter was sleeping between two soldiers, bound with two chains: and the keepers before the door kept the prison* (Acts 12:4-6).

It looked like a hopeless and dead-end circumstance, literally. Nothing could be done naturally. There was no connection and authority in the natural that could deliver Peter. This death assignment looked like it was going ahead full throttle! The church had a different idea though. They tapped into *unceasing prayer.* Literally, Scripture revealed, *the unceasing prayer was made...* (see Acts 12:5) referring to praying and interceding in tongues, and look at the glorious end result. Herod's death assignment was vetoed, reversed, rescinded, repealed, revoked, disallowed, overrode, quashed, annulled, nullified, invalidated, negated, and made void. I really like the word *invalidated.* This tells me *to be rendered invalid.* Tongues will render your enemy as an invalid against you. This further lets you know that every assignment of wizardry against your life will be vetoed by praying in the spirit. The next time we hear about Herod, he is struck down by the angel of the Lord and being eaten by worms (see Acts 12:23). What a turn of events! Worms should have been eating Peter's body, but they were now eating Herod's body. The death assignment was cancelled and returned to sender by praying in tongues.

Tongues reverses death and demonic assignments against your life.

---

35. *Tongues removes you from the limitations of the flesh and taps into God's abundant supply of the Spirit.*

Your flesh is limited. Your intellect and education, no matter what great institution you attended and gleaned from, will not help you in all of life's complex circumstances. We tend to pull from our education and reasoning faculties to solve problems, and many times we face issues that our doctorate and other degrees will not solve. See what the apostle Paul says concerning his imprisonment, "For I know that this shall turn to my salvation through your prayer, and the supply of the Spirit of Jesus Christ" (Phil. 1:19). He was expecting the situation to turn for and not against him. How? By prayer and the supply of the Spirit. Praying in tongues is your spirit praying by the Holy Spirit. In essence, when you pray in tongues, you are making demands on the supply of the power of God to deliver you. It is the law of demand and supply. If there is no demand, then there will be no supply. Praying in tongues is the demand, and the miracle power of God is the supply.

Tongues is making demands upon the power of God.

---

36. *Praying in tongues enables a closer walk with God.*

Then Peter said unto them, "Repent, and let every one of you be baptized in the name of Jesus Christ for the remission of sins; and you shall receive the gift of the Holy Spirit. For the promise is to you and to your children, and to all who are afar off, as many as the Lord our God will call (Acts 2:38-39 NKJV).

37. *Praying in tongues is speaking the hidden wisdom of God.*

Solomon said that "wisdom is the principal thing" (Prov. 4:7) and that "wisdom is profitable to direct" (Eccles. 10:10). Wisdom is powerful, profitable, and the principal thing because it is the voice of God to direct our lives. Following God's direction for our lives is absolutely crucial to our success in life. How do we tap into that wisdom?

But we speak the wisdom of God in a mystery, even the hidden wisdom, which God ordained before the world unto our glory (1 Corinthians 2:7).

As mentioned previously, Paul said praying in tongues is speaking mysteries in the spirit. We pray the mystery out. The wisdom of God comes to the surface as we pray in the spirit. Praying in tongues connects us with divine mysteries! There are answers to questions that we will get as we pray out the mystery in tongues! The wisdom of God will be revealed to those who pray more in tongues.

38. *Praying in tongues is the beginning of being led by the Spirit.*

Praying in tongues is yielding and showing confidence in the Holy Spirit. The great privilege we have as believers in the New Testament is to be led by the Spirit of God.

> *For as many as are led by the Spirit of God, they are the sons of God. For ye have not received the spirit of bondage again to fear; but ye have received the Spirit of adoption, whereby we cry, Abba, Father. The Spirit itself beareth witness with our spirit, that we are the children of God* (Romans 8:14-16).

Habit becomes our destiny and future. When we develop the habit of praying in tongues, we are developing the habit of surrendering and yielding to God the Holy Ghost. Jesus said, "Howbeit when He, the Spirit of truth, is come, He will guide you into all truth: for He shall not speak of Himself; but whatsoever He shall hear, that shall He speak: and He will shew you things to come" (John 16:13). Praying in tongues is your avenue of being led by the Holy Spirit and Him showing you the future.

Tongues is living supernaturally in a natural world.

Tongues help you to develop your prayer life. The Holy Spirit is the spirit of grace and supplication (see Zech. 12:10) that enables you to pray.

39. *Praying in tongues opens the heavens and charges the atmosphere.*

> *So likewise ye, except ye utter by the tongue words easy to be understood, how shall it be known what is spoken ? for ye shall speak into the air* (1 Corinthians 14:9).

Wherein in time past ye walked according to the course of this world, according to the prince of the power of the air, the spirit that now worketh in the children of disobedience (Ephesians 2:2).

In whom the god of this world hath blinded the minds of them which believe not, lest the light of the glorious gospel of Christ, who is the image of God, should shine unto them (2 Corinthians 4:4).

The word *air* is the Greek word, *aer* meaning "the lower, denser atmosphere." The atmosphere is dominated by the prince of the power of the air, meaning *satan*. Paul is telling us that the trend of the physical world is a result of one who is forcefully pulling the strings in the atmosphere above us. If you want to change the course of the environment in which you live, it is imperative that the heaven over you is open. Paul tells us that everything that happens in the Old Testament serves as an example, figure, a type, and a shadow of things to come for us in the New Testament. Elijah prayed, and the heaven opened, and the rain came down. Moses, in his writings, (see Lev. 26:19-20; Deut. 11:16-17; 28:23-26) also talks about a closed and brass heaven above which results in:

- *Strength spent in vain*, meaning working ever so hard and having nothing to show for it.

- *Land shall not yield increase*, meaning no harvest.

- *Perish quickly*, meaning premature death.

- *Smitten before thine enemies*, meaning abject defeat.

The point is very simple! If the atmosphere above you is closed or shut up, then hardship and calamity follow. Paul tells the Ephesian saints that the battle is against wicked spirits in the heavenlies. (See Ephesians 6:12.) We know there are three heavens.

1. *Heaven where God is, also known as the third heaven.*

2. *The stella heaven, where the stars and planets are, the universe, also known as second heaven.*

3. *The atmosphere above us, also known as the firmament. This is the place where spiritual battles take place.*

Now, here is the extreme value of praying in tongues. Paul declares when we pray in tongues we are speaking into the air. The same word which is used for *atmosphere*. What a powerful thought! Some people today call it *warring tongues*. Tongues, which are words emanating from the Holy Spirit, will charge and create a better atmosphere.

A Lesson Learned From a Visitor

Growing up as a young believer, there were two major things in my life that I constantly pursued after. They were the studying of God's Word and praying in tongues. I loved praying in tongues, and like the apostle Paul, I thank God I speak in tongues. I would spend hours in my bedroom praying in tongues. I also loved to go to all-night prayer meetings and prayed in tongues for hours. My bedroom was my sanctuary. I did not allow any secular music in my room. There was only teaching or the Bible being played in my room, and the constant barrage of praying in tongues. It was a very peaceful room. My mom would say to me many times, "Your room is very peaceful; it has a good atmosphere." I never paid any attention to it.

One time, we had a cousin who visited us from Paris, France. At that time, we lived in a three-bedroom house. I had my own room, and my two brothers shared a bigger room. My mom said to me, "Glenn, tonight you will sleep in your brother's bedroom, and your cousin will sleep in your room." Well, I didn't think anything about it. I said "Yes, sure." Little did we know that the cousin was demon possessed. I woke up to the sound of her voice screaming like a man. She ran to my mom's bedroom saying, "I cannot sleep in that room! I AM NOT GOING TO SLEEP IN THAT ROOM!"

We were all young Christians! We tried to cast the devil out of her! My mom said, "Come out of her devil!"

She yelled back, "No!"

When she said no, my mother looked perplexed and said, "What!" and then slapped her.

Then, my father said, "No, no, no, let me do it."

He came and commanded, and that devil screamed, "Nooooo," to which then my dad slapped her on the cheek. We had never cast out a devil before. After my mom and dad, then it was my two brothers. They also slapped her. James, my youngest brother who was ten at the time, slapped her more out of fear and to get her to snap out of it, but to no avail. I came in, commanded, and she screamed and refused, so I slapped her too. Now that is not how you cast out devils.

We had to call my uncle Tony, who had led us to the Lord. He came to the house at 3 A.M. and cast that stinking devil out. Otherwise, we would have slapped her until she snapped out of it. Thank God we have grown up spiritually now. Now think about this! The atmosphere in the room disturbed the devil in her. The atmosphere was charged by praying in tongues. What do you think will happen if your entire church congregation prayed in tongues? The atmosphere of the church will be electrified and demons will not be able to stay in your midst. There will be manifestations of healings and deliverances. Charge your atmosphere! *Praying in tongues is creating an atmosphere for the release of the shekinah glory.* Praying in tongues is pressing in the heavenlies to do damage to enemy forces in the hostile clash between darkness and light. It is establishing a spiritual climate and atmosphere in regions that becomes conducive for the release of the glory of God.

Tongues opens the heavens and creates an atmosphere for the release of the shekinah glory.

---

40. Praying in tongues is getting drunk on the new wine of the Holy Ghost.

And be not drunk with wine, wherein is excess; but be filled with the Spirit (Ephesians 5:18).

Don't drink too much wine. That cheapens your life. Drink the Spirit of God, huge draughts of Him (Ephesians 5:18 TM).

And it came to pass, that, while Apollos was at Corinth, Paul having passed through the upper coasts came to Ephesus: and finding certain disciples, he said unto them, Have ye received the Holy Ghost since ye believed? And they said unto him, We have not so much as heard whether there be any Holy Ghost. And he said unto them, Unto what then were ye baptized? And they said, Unto John's baptism. Then said Paul, John verily baptized with the baptism of repentance, saying unto the people, that they should believe on Him which should come after him, that is, on Christ Jesus. When they heard this, they were baptized in the name of the Lord Jesus. And when Paul had laid his hands upon them, the Holy Ghost came on them; and they spake with tongues, and prophesied (Acts 19:1-6).

Tongues is pouring in the oil and wine of the Holy Ghost.

When Paul first passed through Ephesus, we see he prayed for the Ephesians saints to be baptized and filled with the Holy Ghost with the evidence of speaking in other tongues. Then years later in his epistles to the same saints, Paul commands, "Be not drunk with wine...but be filled with the Spirit" (Eph. 5:18). Why would he command them to be filled with the Spirit if they were already filled? The answer is clearer when we look at the original text which reads, "But be being filled." The Amplified Bible fitly translates this verse, "And do not get drunk with wine, for that is debauchery; but ever be filled and stimulated with the [Holy] Spirit." Being filled with the Holy Ghost is not a one time event; it is a continuous event. Just like on the day of Pentecost, when they were baptized and spoke in tongues, they were accused of being drunk by the people.

*Others mocking said, These men are full of new wine. But
Peter, standing up with the eleven, lifted up his voice, and
said unto them, Ye men of Judaea, and all ye that dwell at
Jerusalem, be this known unto you, and hearken to my
words: For these are not drunken, as ye suppose, seeing it
is but the third hour of the day. But this is that which was
spoken by the prophet Joel; And it shall come to pass in
the last days, saith God, I will pour out of My Spirit upon
all flesh (Acts 2:13-17).*

There is a term used in Hermeneutics called *The Law of First
Mention*, which simply means that the very first time any important
word or occurrence is mentioned in the Scripture, it gives that word
its most complete, and accurate meaning to not only serve as a key in
understanding the word's biblical concept, but to also provide a
foundation for its fuller development in the latter parts of the Scripture. An easier way to explain this principle of biblical interpretation
is to say *the first time a subject is mentioned, the subject remains un-
changed throughout Scripture.* The Book of Acts is the genesis of the
New Covenant or Testament.

Isn't it interesting that on the day of Pentecost when the Holy
Spirit made His grand descent in the earth and came upon the disciples, it is mentioned that they spoke in tongues and were viewed as
drunk with new wine. Then, Paul used the same analogy for admon-
ishing all to keep being filled and refilled with the Holy Spirit. How
do we do that? By praying and tapping into the power of praying in
tongues. What the Church needs today is the new wine of the Holy
Ghost. Now look at what Paul said further, "For the kingdom of
God is not meat and drink; but righteousness, and peace, and joy in
the Holy Ghost" (Rom. 14:17). Righteous, peace, and joy in the
Holy Ghost. That's what happens when the believer receives Christ
and is saved. First he is justified and made righteous by the shed
blood of the Lord Jesus. The result is he now has peace with God, is
no longer an alien or enemy of His; and third, he becomes the habi-
tat of the Holy Spirit, which is joy unspeakable and full of glory. Joy
in the Holy Ghost is the new wine of the Holy Ghost. Praying in
tongues will stir the the wine of the Spirit to keep you joyful. You
cannot be depressed when the joy of the Holy Ghost is in your life.

The Scripture states, "The joy of the Lord is your strength" (Neh. 8:10) and when joy is in your life, you will be strong. The reason so many believers' Christianity is dry is due to the fact that they are not drunk on the new wine of the Spirit. The new wine of the Holy Ghost will make your Christian life an adventure.

ENDNOTE

1. Strong's Concordance #H1254, s.v. *bara*.

Chapter 6

BENEFITS OF PRAYING
IN TONGUES (41-60)

By now you should be as enthused as the apostle Paul and declare, "I thank my God, I speak with tongues more than ye all." (See First Corinthians 14:18.) Like great ministers such as John G. Lake, Smith Wigglesworth, and Oral Roberts, tongues will be the making of you and your ministry. As you consistently meditate and act upon these listed benefits, you will see great advancement in your life. Let us look at more impartations that you can receive from the power of praying in tongues.

41. Praying in tongues is faith-filled words and anointing-filled words to dominate the law of sin and death.

> *For the law of the Spirit of life in Christ Jesus hath made me free from the law of sin and death* (Romans 8:2).

The whole world system is under the sway of the law of sin and death. This law is keeping people in the bondage of sin and the curse of the law is operating on a worldwide scale causing havoc in the lives of people. Thank God for the Spirit of life who elevates our lives above the mayhem in this world. Praying in tongues keeps our close connection to the Spirit of life stirred to live above the curses of the world. Solomon said, life and death are in the power of the tongue and that we are snared by the words of our mouth. (See Proverbs 18:21, Proverbs 6:2.) Praying in tongues is life-filled words, faith-filled words, and anointing-filled words to dominate the law of sin and death. Praying in tongues does not snare our lives but releases words of life to bless our lives.

Tongues is life-filled words, faith-filled words, and anointing-filled words.

---

42. *Praying in tongues rekindles the fire of God in your life.*

John the Baptist said, "I indeed baptized you with water unto repentance but there is One coming who is mightier than me, whose shoes I am not worthy to bear and **He will baptize you with the Holy Ghost and fire**" (see Matt. 3:11-12). On the day of Pentecost, there was cloven tongues of fire that sat upon their heads "and they were all filled with the Holy Ghost, and began to speak with other tongues, as the Spirit gave them utterance" (Acts 2:3-4). Paul emphasized to the Thessalonians not to "quench the Spirit," which is synonymous to him saying to the Corinthians, "Forbid not to speak with tongues" (1 Cor. 14:39). *To quench* in Greek is *sbennymi* and means "to extinguish the fire out."[1] When we forbid praying in tongues, we are extinguishing the fire of God from our lives. Other translations of Paul's command to the Thessalonians are very enlightening:

Do *not put out the Spirit's fire* (1 Thessalonians 5:19 NIV).

Do *not quench (suppress or subdue) the [Holy] Spirit* (1 Thessalonians 5:19 AMP).

Tongues lights the fire of God in your life.

Fire is important for the believer, the minister, and the church. See what God instructs, "Meanwhile, the fire on the altar must be kept burning; it must never go out. Each morning the priest will add fresh wood to the fire..." (see Lev. 6:12 NLT). God has said that the fire must never be put out! That is what praying in tongues does; it keeps the fire lit on the altar. Many Christians are stuck with cold altars because they never pray in the spirit. Allow me to remind you that God is still the God who answers by fire. He is a consuming fire. Moses saw Him as a burning bush. He is the refiner's fire. God is the pillar of fire by night. He is a fire from the loins up, to the loins down. The Book of Revelation describes Jesus as having flames of fire in his eyes. Now I want you to check this very important story in the Old Testament and how it applies to your life:

> *Now king David was old and stricken in years; and they covered him with clothes, but he gat no heat. Wherefore his servants said unto him, Let there be sought for my lord the king a young virgin: and let her stand before the king, and let her cherish him, and let her lie in thy bosom, that my lord the king may get heat. So they sought for a fair damsel throughout all the coasts of Israel, and found Abishag a Shunammite, and brought her to the king. And the damsel was very fair, and cherished the king, and ministered to him: but the king knew her not* (1 Kings 1:1-4).

Keep the Fire in Your Latter Years

The great King David was now advanced in age and living at the end of his life. He could not keep himself warm. There was no more fire in his bones and body. David, who was a mighty warrior in his youth, could not keep himself warm in his old years. That is the same for many believers. It is amazing how many new Christians are on fire when they first get saved, but as time goes by many lose their fire and become lukewarm. They have no heat, no fire in their later years—just going through the motion of church, but there is no life, no vibrancy in their walk with God. If a believer is on fire, you will know it. Fire purifies, and fire is an attraction. As you pray in tongues, it will purify your life and draw the power and life of God to your life. The more you pray in tongues, the more you are fanning the flame of the Spirit in your life. Praying in tongues ignites and maintains revival fires in your life, home, church, community, city, and country.

Praying in tongues will deliver you from the scourge of the tongue.

---

43. *Praying in tongues will shake your prison doors open.*

> *And at midnight Paul and Silas prayed, and sang praises unto God: and the prisoners heard them. And suddenly there was a great earthquake, so that the foundations of the prison were shaken: and immediately all the doors were opened, and every one's bands were loosed. And the keeper of the prison awaking out of his sleep, and seeing the prison doors open, he drew out his sword, and would have killed himself, supposing that the prisoners had been fled* (Acts 16:25-27).

Paul and Silas were arrested, beaten, and thrown in jail for preaching the Gospel. Their backs were bleeding and their feet were in stocks. They could have felt sorry for themselves, but instead they chose to pray. Their prayer led to singing praises. True prayer always leads to praise. Then the prison doors shot wide open and all the chains fell off. This is what praying in tongues will do for you. Every chain in your life will fall off. All doors that the devil has shut in your face will be opened. I see doors of opportunities opening for you as you pray in the Holy Ghost. I see doors of miracles opening for you. I see all closed doors opened as you kick them wide open through praying in tongues. As Paul declared to the Corinthian believers, "Where the Spirit of the Lord is, there is liberty" (2 Cor. 3:17).

Tongues unlocks doors that have been shut in your face.

---

44. *Praying in tongues is a well springing up into everlasting life.*

> *But whosoever drinketh of the water that I shall give him shall never thirst; but the water that I shall give him shall be in him a well of water springing up into everlasting life* (John 4:14).

Water is one of our world's major commodities. Jesus said that there is a well inside the believer. Wells played an important role in biblical times. Jacob's well is where the Samaritan woman discovered the Messiah, Jesus. (See John 4.) We know that Isaac dug the wells of his father Abraham. What is interesting about a well in ancient times is that when a person had one, he would no longer have to keep moving and relocating. The well would settle the family and meet their private needs. Families would fight great fights over wells. We see there was constant friction between the Philistines and Isaac because of wells. A well meant survival. It was for private use. Solomon validates this thought in his writing, "Drink waters out of thine own cistern, and running waters out of thine own well" (Prov. 5:15). Praying in tongues is a well inside of us for private use. When we pray in tongues, we are drawing water of life to refresh our lives. Tongues is tapping into the spring that the Holy Spirit has deposited into our spirit. It will meet our needs and bring much refreshing in our lives.

Tongues means refreshment and rest.

---

45. *Praying in tongues is the beginning and the maintaining of partnership with the Holy Spirit.*

The grace of the Lord Jesus Christ, and the love of God, and the communion of the Holy Ghost, be with you all. Amen (2 Corinthians 13:14).

Look at these words, *"the communion of the Holy Ghost be with you all."* The word *communion* is the Greek word *koinonia*, and it conveys the thought of partnership and intimacy.[2] Today, when we hear the word *partnership*, we can get the idea of just a cold and legal merger of two business partners who have nothing in common. Their partnership is only for business and the relationship goes no further. *Koinonia* is different! It is a relationship that has been cultivated and cherished through fellowship and time that builds into a firm friendship. The fellowship and the time builds the trust. Jesus also said, "But when the Comforter is come, whom I will send unto you from the Father, even the Spirit of truth..." (John 15:26). The Holy Spirit with whom we are to develop a partnership is also called the *Comforter*. This word is *parakletos* in the Greek language and it is a combination of two words, *para* meaning "alongside"; the idea is standing side by side.[3]

Second, the word *kletos* comes from *kaleo* meaning "called." So, the two words combined mean "called to stand side by side." The word *parakletos* was also used to refer to someone representing and pleading your case in court. The Holy Spirit is not only in you, but He also wants to stand with you. I really love the way the Amplified Bible gives us the sevenfold meaning of the word *parakletos*. It means "Advocate, Counselor, Comforter, Helper, Intercessor, Strengthener and Standby." The believer is to have *koinonia* with the *parakletos*. You are to have a close relationship with the Spirit of God. This is done when you begin to pray in tongues. First of all, you had to trust the Holy Spirit to give you the utterance in tongues, and the more you pray in tongues on a daily basis, the more you are developing friendship and partnership with Him. In fact, this is the purpose behind praying in tongues. It is for you to develop a close relationship with God. There are two major ways to know God. Through the study of His Word and fellowshipping or partnering with Him in prayer. When you pray in tongues, you are maintaining a close link to the Holy Spirit.

Tongues is Koinonia with the Parakletos.

---

46. *Praying in tongues is releasing the winds of God to blow in our lives.*

> *And when the day of Pentecost was fully come, they were all with one accord in one place. And suddenly there came a sound from heaven as of a rushing mighty wind, and it filled all the house where they were sitting* (Acts 2:1-2).

There is supernatural manifestation of greatness when God's wind is moving in a situation. You will remember when God showed the prophet Ezekiel a valley of dry bones, which represented the house of Israel, the bones were dried because they had been in a state of death for a long time; but God told Ezekiel to prophesy to death, and look at what happened:

> *Then said He unto me, Prophesy unto the wind, prophesy, son of man, and say to the wind, Thus saith the Lord God; Come from the four winds, O breath, and breathe upon these slain, that they may live. So I prophesied as He commanded me, and the breath came into them, and they lived, and stood up upon their feet, an exceeding great army* (Ezekiel 37:9-10).

God told Ezekiel to prophesy to the four winds to bring life to these dead dry bones. Notice there are four winds that the Bible talks about. They are the East Wind, West Wind, South Wind, and North Wind.

A. The East Wind

Israel had already left Egypt, but now Pharaoh and his host were after them. Behind them was Pharaoh and in front of them was the Red Sea. They were stuck in the middle. The sea was the barrier and obstacle that would surely bring death to them and their young ones. By this conclusion, the children of Israel were beside themselves in fear and moaning at Moses. He called upon God and look at what God did, "And Moses stretched out his hand over the sea: and the Lord caused the sea to go back by a strong east wind all that night and made the sea dry land and the waters were divided (Exod. 14:21). God used the East wind to remove the barrier stopping His children from moving forward. The East wind is the wind of destruction and judgement to every barrier in your life. The East wind was also the one that brought the plague of locusts over Pharaoh and Egypt.

B. The West Wind

Egypt was under the plague and swarm of locust. It was so dense that it made the country dark. There was total devastation of crops, and harvest was totally destroyed in all of Egypt. When Pharaoh saw all of his nation's GDP gone, he repented and Moses asked God's mercy over the land and God sent the West wind of mercy and grace.

> *Then Pharaoh called for Moses and Aaron in haste; and he said, I have sinned against the Lord your God, and against you. Now therefore forgive, I pray thee, my sin only this once, and intreat the Lord your God, that he may take away from me this death only. And he went out from Pharaoh, and **intreated** the Lord. And the Lord turned a mighty strong west wind, which took away the locusts, and cast them into the Red sea; there remained not one locust in all the coasts of Egypt (Exodus 10:16-19).*

C. The South Wind

The South wind is a soft, gentle, and warm wind of provision and destination. Jesus talked about the South wind, "...when ye see the south wind blow, ye say, There will be heat; and it cometh to pass" (Luke 12:55).

Luke, the beloved physician also gives us a revelation of this wind,

> *And when the south wind blew softly, supposing that they had obtained their purpose, loosing thence, they sailed close by Crete (Acts 27:13).*

> *And from thence we fetched a compass, and came to Rhegium: and after one day the south wind blew, and we came the next day to Puteoli (Acts 28:13).*

> *...And by His power he brought in the south wind. He rained flesh also upon them as dust, and feathered fowls like as the sand of the sea: And he let it fall in the midst of their camp, round about their habitations. So they did eat, and were well filled (Psalm 78:26-29).*

I see the South wind blowing in your life and taking you into your destiny. The storm is over! The turmoil is over. The delay is over! Enter into your destiny.

D. North Wind

> *Awake, O north wind; and come, thou south; blow upon my garden, that the spices thereof may flow out. Let my beloved come into his garden, and eat his pleasant fruits* (Song of Solomon 4:16).

The North Wind is a wind of vibrant growth and harvest. May God blow upon your garden so that spices may flow and that there is a great harvest of fruit. The North wind will destroy barrenness out of your life. This wind will make you fruitful and your life an aroma of joy.

The Holy Ghost made His entrance as a rushing mighty wind, and they then began to speak in other tongues. The winds of God, the Holy Spirit, are for revival, renewal, refreshing, resurrection, and rejuvenation.

As you pray in tongues, every barrier in your life will be blown by the winds of God.

As you pray in tongues, the wind of fruitfulness will blow over your life. Barrenness and frustration in ministry will be a thing of the past.

As you pray in tongues, the wind of destiny is blowing you into your safe haven.

As you pray in tongues, the wind of mercy, favor, and grace is over your life.

As you pray in tongues, the wind of God's abundant provision will break the yoke of poverty out of your life. Pray in tongues and release the four mighty rushing winds of God in your life.

Tongues unleashes the winds of revival and refreshing in your life.

---

47. *Tongues is building a building to carry the anointing.*

The anointing is a heavenly responsibility that ministers and believers have to carry to a lost and dying world. Unfortunately, many believers as well as ministers do not know how to be an anointed vessel to release the glory and virtue of God. The more we pray in the Spirit, the more we are building our spirits to release the power of God. Tongues will build in you a house of power. We can learn a great lesson from when Jesus walked into the temple.

> *And Jesus went into the temple of God, and cast out all them that sold and bought in the temple, and overthrew the tables of the moneychangers, and the seats of them that sold doves, And said unto them, It is written, My house shall be called the house of prayer; but ye have made it a den of thieves. And the blind and the lame came to Him in the temple; and He healed them (Matthew 21:12-14).*

This event literally happened two thousand years ago, but this is also a picture of what happens when a sinner receives Christ. Jesus then comes into our temple and cleanses us from all unrighteousness thereby making us a pure house. After purifying and cleansing the temple, our Lord states that the house that has been cleansed and purified is to be a house of prayer. This is paramount as we then see that the lame and blind came into the temple and were healed. Notice, after being designated the house of prayer, the temple became the house of power and miracles. The house of prayer becomes the house of anointing to heal the sick. This is why we must continuously pray in tongues—so that we can be the house of power and anointing to minister to this miracle-starved world.

Tongues builds you into the house of the anointing.

---

48. *Praying in tongues is new wine for new wineskin.*

> *Neither do men put new wine into old bottles: else the bottles break, and the wine runneth out, and the bottles perish: but they put new wine into new bottles, and both are preserved (Matthew 9:17).*

The new wineskin is the recreated human spirit by faith in the blood of Christ. The new wine is the Holy Ghost. On the day of Pentecost, the disciples after speaking in tongues as the Spirit gave them utterance, were accused, "These men are full of new wine" (Acts 2:13). Isn't it interesting that they used the term *new wine*. Tongues is the new wine of the Holy Ghost. As you pray in tongues on a daily basis, you will fill up on the new wine of the Spirit from which there is no hangover.

Tongues is filling the empty vessel.

---

49. *Tongues is spirit-to-Spirit communication.*

Jesus said that God is a Spirit, but He is more than that. See what the author of Hebrews penned:

> *Furthermore we have had fathers of our flesh which corrected us, and we gave them reverence: shall we not much rather be in subjection unto the Father of spirits, and live?* (Hebrews 12:9)

God is the Father of spirits. As a creature made after His image, we are also spirits. In fact, humankind is a tripartite being consisting of spirit, soul, and body (see 1 Thess. 5:23). As important as the flesh is, yet, it is only the suit of the real man, the spirit. The body needs the spirit to live, but the spirit does not need the body to live. James in his epistle reveals, "...the body without the spirit is dead..." (James 2:26). Man is a spirit, and God is a Spirit. Paul narrates to the Corinthians, "For if I pray in an [unknown] tongue, my spirit [by the Holy Spirit within me] prays..." (1 Cor. 14:14 AMP). Praying in tongues is spirit-to-Spirit communication. It is you, the child-spirit, communicating to your Father, the Father of spirits. Jesus said, "God is a Spirit and they that worship Him *must* worship Him in spirit and in truth" (John 4:24). The word *must* means "obliged to." This is not optional, but a prerequisite. Praying in tongues is my spirit communicating and woshiping my Father in spirit and in truth.

50. *Praying in tongues is living effectively in the last days. It is God's antidote for the spirit of fear.*

> *But, beloved, remember ye the words which were spoken before of the apostles of our Lord Jesus Christ; How that they told you there should be mockers in the last time, who should walk after their own ungodly lusts. These be*

they who separate themselves, sensual, having not the Spirit. But ye, beloved, building up yourselves on your most holy faith, praying in the Holy Ghost (Jude 1:17-20).

We know that the last days began on the day of Pentecost, as Peter said that which happend was a fulfillment of Joel's prophetic utterance, "...this is that which was spoken by the prophet Joel; And it shall come to pass **in the last days**, saith God, I will pour out of My Spirit upon all flesh: and your sons and your daughters shall prophesy, and your young men shall see visions, and your old men shall dream dreams" (Acts 2:16-17). The last days began on the day of Pentecost and over 2,000 years have transpired since that day which can only bring us to this conclusion that we are now living in the last of the last days. Paul told us that in the last days there will be perilous times.

This know also, that in the last days perilous times shall come. For men shall be lovers of their own selves, covetous, boasters, proud, blasphemers, disobedient to parents, unthankful, unholy, Without natural affection, trucebreakers, false accusers, incontinent, fierce, despisers of those that are good, Traitors, heady, highminded, lovers of pleasures more than lovers of God; Having a form of godliness, but denying the power thereof: from such turn away (2 Timothy 3:1-5).

It does not take great insights for us to realize that we are living in perilous times. These are the last days. The news media reports calamities and horrific circumstances every day. These are days that inspire fear in people's lives. In fact, Jesus said, "Men's hearts will fail them for fear and for looking upon those things which are coming on the earth; for the powers of heaven shall be shaken" (Luke 21:26). How are the believers supposed to live in these days? Are we supposed to bury our heads in the sand like these things are not happening? Not so! In the midst of calamities and fearful days, God expects us to walk in victory. How do we do that; and more importantly, while everybody is collapsing, how does the believer live effectively in the last days? Jude provides the answer:

- Build your faith—walk by faith and not by sight.

- Pray in the Holy Ghost—develop the habit of praying in tongues.

- Keep yourselves in the love of God—walk in love.

Notice that praying in the Holy Ghost is an effective tool to live in the last days. It is God's antidote for the spirit of fear. Praying in tongues will build and stimulate your faith. When faith is present, fear crouches. Praying in tongues is a major weapon to stop the spirit of fear from running rampant in the last days and to prevent it from overwhelming and taking over your life.

Tongues is living effectively in the last days.

---

51. *Praying in tongues is the ignition to walking in the power of God.*

> *But you shall receive power when the Holy Spirit is come upon you; and you shall be witnesses unto Me in Jerusalem, and in all Judea, and Samaria, and to the end of the earth* (Acts 1:8 NKJV).

There is a dual work of the Holy Spirit in the life of the believer—the Spirit *within* and the Spirit *upon*. When the believer receives Christ at the new birth, he is indwelt by the Holy Spirit, but when the Spirit comes upon the believer, it is for the manifestation of supernatural power. It is to be endued with power from on high. Jesus told the disciples not go anywhere or do anything until they were clothed with power from on high. On the day of Pentecost, they were clothed with power and they spoke in tongues and became fearless witnesses and workers of God's miracles in the earth.The Holy Spirit coming *within* you was for your personal benefit. The Holy Spirit coming *upon* you is for the benefit of others. We receive assurance personally from the indwelling of the Holy Spirit. But we are divinely and supernaturally enabled to be powerful witnesses through the Holy Spirit coming upon us. See the testimony of the apostle Paul:

"For I will not dare to speak of anything except what Christ has accomplished through me in order to bring about the obedience of the

Gentiles, by word and deed, **in the power of signs and wonders, in the power of the Spirit of God.** So from Jerusalem even as far as Illyricum I have fully preached the gospel of Christ." (See Romans 15:18-19.)

Tongues is to be endued with dunamis from on high.

---

52. *Praying in tongues is rivers of living water flowing out of you.*

He that believeth on Me, as the scripture hath said, out of his belly shall flow rivers of living water (John 7:38).

Praying in tongues causes the rivers of God to flow out of you to meet all your needs. There is a difference between a well and a river. A well is for private use; whereas, a river crosses through the nation and some through to other nations. The more a believer prays in the Holy Ghost, the more living waters will flow out of him or her. The more you increase in the flow of water, the more increase in the anointing to be a blessing to other people. As you pray and increase in tongues, it will bring you to a place where others will be blessed by your life.

Tongues is drinking from the river and reservoir of God.

---

53. *Praying in tongues is serving God in your spirit.*

For God is my witness, whom I serve with my spirit in the gospel of his Son, that without ceasing I make mention of you always in my prayers (Romans 1:9).

The Holy Spirit is the Source of living water. Both John and Ezekiel talk about the river of God. "Then he showed me a river of the water of life, clear as crystal, coming from the throne of God and of the Lamb, in the middle of its street. On either side of the river was the tree of life, bearing twelve kinds of fruit, yielding its fruit every month; and the leaves of the tree were for the healing of the nations" (see Rev. 22:1-2 NASB).

Tongues helps you to enjoy the vital side of our new birth as as children of God, whereas the Word opens us to the legal side.

---

54. *Praying in tongues enables you to perform your priestly function.*

> *And from Jesus Christ, who is the faithful witness, and the first begotten of the dead, and the prince of the kings of the earth. Unto Him that loved us, and washed us from our sins in His own blood, And **hath made us kings and priests unto God and His Father;** to Him be glory and dominion for ever and ever. Amen* (Revelation 1:5-6).

All believers get excited about being kings! The majority of today's preaching concentrates on our authority and power as appointed kings, but very few focus on the priesthood part. The function of a priest is to be an intermediary between God and people. Priests represent the people to God! Priests intercede! As constituted priests, it is our duty to pray and intercede. We can see this in the priesthood of Jesus.

> *But this Man, because He continueth ever, hath an **unchangeable priesthood.** Wherefore He is able also to save them to the uttermost that come unto God by Him, **seeing he ever liveth to make intercession for them*** (Hebrews 7:24-25).

Christ Jesus has an unchangeable priesthood and it involves unending prayers of intercession. We see the sacred duties in the life of Zachariah, who was also a priest and the father of John the Baptist. He was serving as priest before God when his division was on duty. According to the custom of the priesthood, he was chosen by lot to enter the temple of the Lord and burn incense. And the whole multitude of the people were praying outside at the hour of incense. For us today, this is where praying in tongues takes its prominent place. See what the apostle Paul says:

Likewise the Spirit also helpeth our infirmities: for we know not what we should pray for as we ought: but the Spirit itself maketh intercession for us with groanings which cannot be uttered. And He that searcheth the hearts knoweth what is the mind of the Spirit, because He maketh intercession for the saints according to the will of God (Romans 8:26-27).

Praying in tongues is the Holy Spirit interceding through us and for us. Praying in tongues is interceding to bring in the mind of God on the earth. As we pray in tongues, we are interceding and fulfilling our priestly duties through the Holy Ghost.

Tongues is intercession and fulfilling our priestly duties.

---

55. *Praying in tongues builds your confidence.*

But ye beloved, building up yourselves on your most holy faith, praying in the Holy Ghost (Jude 1:20).

But you, dear friends, carefully build yourselves up in this most holy faith by praying in the Holy Spirit... (Jude 1:20 TM).

This is an interesting verse. Many times we miss out on what the Word is saying because we become familiar with the Scriptures and assume that we already know all about what a particular verse is saying. Many who have read this verse have simply concluded that this verse is just saying that we build our spirits by praying in the Holy Ghost. This is very true, but not the whole truth. The word *build* also means "encourage." When Jude employed the word *yourselves*, it referred to the totality of humankind. This would mean spirit, soul, and body. Praying in tongues affects all areas of your life. It will definitely affect and encourage your confidence level. First of all, tongues is showing your confidence in the Holy Spirit in stepping into the unknown. Second, it will build your own confidence. It will remove fear of the unknown and fear of people and the future.

114

Tongues is expressing, declaring, and enforcing the will of God in your life, the atmosphere and the earth.

---

56. *Praying in tongues is tuning into the mind of God.*

People are fretting over situations and circumstances. Many are not sleeping or facing separation from their loved ones because of no answer to life's difficulties. The pressures of living life with no answer can get overwhelming for many. The thing that you must realize is that whatever is troubling you is not troubling God. Whatever is disturbing you and causing you to fret, is not disturbing Him in the least. Why? Because God knows what to do about your situation. The reason you are worried and under pressure is because you do not know what God knows. If you knew what He knew, you would be just like Him. Through praying in tongues, you access the mind of God, which will bring peace to your life.

Tongues is extracting answers from the indwelling spirit to solve life's problems.

---

57. *Praying in tongues is allowing my spirit to pray and lifting the shield of faith to quench fiery darts.*

Paul declared to the believers in Corinth, "For if I pray in an unknown tongue, my spirit prayeth, but my understanding is unfruitful. What is it then? I will pray with the spirit, and I will pray with the understanding also: I will sing with the spirit, and I will sing with the understanding also" (1 Cor. 14:14-15). It is a conscious decision on Paul's behalf to pray from his spirit man. This was a function of his will. There are people today who advocate that we can only pray in tongues when we feel inspired. That goes completely against what Paul says when he writes, "I will pray with my spirit, I will sing with my spirit" (see 1 Cor. 14:15). Paul also states, "I thank my God that **I speak** in tongues more than ye all" (see 1 Cor. 14:18). Notice the words, *I speak*. He didn't say *when I felt inspired or something pushed me*. Praying in tongues is just as simple as turning your water faucet on and off. It is for your devotions and private satisfaction.

115

Now Paul in writing to the Ephesians declared, "Above all lifting up the shield of faith which is able to quench the fiery darts of the wicked one" (see Eph. 6:16). The darts of satan are flaming, and what will quench them is water. Jesus said, "Out of your belly shall flow rivers of living water" (see John 7:38). So, praying in tongues releases the waters of the Holy Ghost to quench the flaming arrows of the devil in your life.

Praying in tongues is the key to igniting revival in a church and community.

---

58. Praying in tongues is giving ascendency of your spirit over your flesh.

> *For he that soweth to his flesh shall of the flesh reap corruption; but he that soweth to the Spirit shall of the Spirit reap life everlasting* (Galatians 6:8).

> *For if ye live after the flesh, ye shall die: but if ye through the Spirit do mortify the deeds of the body, ye shall live* (Romans 8:13).

To mortify means to subdue the body or its needs and desires by discipline. Praying in tongues requires discipline, and our flesh does not like discipline. Our flesh with its passions and cravings likes to dominate our lives. Many believers are so carnal and driven by uncontrolled desires, which gives rise to the works of the flesh to dominate their lives. The weakest a believer will ever be is when the flesh is controlling his or her life, and the strongest a believer will ever be is when the flesh is at its weakest point. This is not in any way referring to sickness or malaise but denial of fleshly cravings. A strong spirit means a weak flesh, and a weak spirit suggests a strong flesh. The more you pray in tongues, the more you give your spirit the ascendency over your flesh.

> *A person without self-control is like a city with broken-down walls* (Proverbs 25:28 NLT).

> *He that hath no rule over his own spirit is like a city that is broken down, and without walls* (Proverbs 25:28).

A spirit-filled believer needs to spend time praying in the spirit to discipline the flesh under control. The very first thing that the believer will gain control over is speaking in tongues. The apostle James stated that if we can control the tongue, we can then gain mastery over the body. Now look at what the Lord told the disciples in the hour of His greatest need:

> *Watch and pray, that ye enter not into temptation: the spirit indeed is willing, but the flesh is weak* (Matthew 26:41).

> *And when He was at the place, He said unto them, Pray that ye enter not into temptation. And said unto them, Why sleep ye? rise and pray, lest ye enter into temptation* (Luke 22:40,46).

We see clearly from the mouth of our Master that the disciples' spirits were weak compared to their flesh, and it resulted in being susceptible to temptations. Praying in tongues edifies the believer to be spiritually strong to resist the temptations of the flesh, the world, and the devil.

Tongues aids the believer to mortify the deeds of the flesh.

---

59. *Praying in tongues connects the intercession of the parakletos in us and our Great High Priest in Heaven to birth the purposes of God in the earth.*

It is the highest form of the prayer of agreement. Many years ago, John Wesley said, "It seems that God will not do anything unless His people pray." Jesus is our mediator who stands between us and the Father God. See what the Book of Hebrews says, "Wherefore He is able also to save them to the uttermost that come unto God by Him, seeing He ever liveth to make intercession for them" (Heb. 7:25).

> *For there is one God, and one mediator between God and men, the man Christ Jesus* (1 Timothy 2:5).

In His high priestly office ministry, Jesus stands before God the Father on our behalf making intercession for us. As I already mentioned, Jesus called the Holy Spirit our Comforter, which in Greek is *parakletos*. The Amplified Bible gives us the sevenfold meaning of the word *parakletos*: "Advocate, Counselor, Comforter, Helper, Intercessor, Strengthener and Standby." Notice that *parakletos* is also an intercessor, and He is in us on the earth. I want you to notice what Jesus said in the Epistle of John:

> *And I will pray the Father, and He shall give you another Comforter, that He may abide with you for ever"* (John 14:16).

The word *another* is the Greek word *allos*, meaning "one exact in kind and character." So our Lord Jesus was also a Comforter—a parakletos, and He sent one just like Him in character. When we pray in tongues, the Holy Spirit, who is the Parakletos-intercessor on earth in us, connects with the heavenly *parakletos-intercessor* Jesus and agrees with Him concerning the will of God, and the purposes and plans of God for our lives.

Tongues is the agreement of the prayers of our earthly and heavenly intercessor with the plan of the Father.

---

60. *Praying in tongues is the threefold cord that will not be broken.*

> "...*And a threefold cord is not quickly broken*" (Ecclesiastes 4:12).

> "...*A cord of three strands is not quickly broken*" (Ecclesiastes 4:12 NIV).

Three is the number of resurrection in the Bible; for Christ Jesus was raised on the third day. Praying in tongues has a threefold scope that is of vital importance to the believer. It will bring resurrection and a quickening in your life.

A. *Praying in tongues is ministering unto the Lord.* The apostle Paul already said, "For he that speaketh in a tongue speaketh not unto men, but unto God..." (1 Cor. 14:2). Also notice that Paul and Barnabas were among those who worshiped and ministered to the Lord, "Now there were in the church that was at Antioch certain prophets and teachers; as Barnabas, and Simeon that was called Niger, and Lucius of Cyrene, and Manaen, which had been brought up with Herod the tetrarch, and Saul. As they ministered to the Lord, and fasted, the Holy Ghost..." (Acts 13:1-2). Paul further declared, "...I will sing with the spirit....For thou verily givest thanks well..." (1 Cor. 14:15,17). The Book of Acts declares tongues as "the wonderful works of God" (Acts 2:11).

B. Praying in tongues is ministering unto yourself. Tongues not only ministers to the Lord but to you. You receive personal benefits from partaking of this great blessing. Look at these four different renderings of what Paul told us would happen when the believer prays in tongues:

> *He that speaketh in an unknown tongue edifieth himself...* (1 Corinthians 14:4).

> *...edifies and improves himself...* (1 Corinthians 14:4 AMP).

> *He who speaks in an unknown tongue does good to himself...* (1 Corinthians 14:4 Weymouth).

> *...Those who speak in strange tongues help only themselves...* (1 Corinthians 14:4 GNB).

C. Praying in tongues is ministering unto others. It enables us to pray for the needs of others in intercession, standing in the gap for their victory.

> *Praying always with all prayer and supplication in the spirit, and watching thereunto with all perseverance and supplication for all saints* (Ephesians 6:18).

Tongues is ministering to yourself, to the Lord, and unto others.

In closing this chapter, praying in tongues enables you to be God-sensitive rather than seeker-sensitive.

We are living in the last of the last days, and the apostle Paul made an interesting observation:

> *This know also, that in the last days perilous times shall come. For men shall be lovers of their own selves, covetous, boasters, proud, blasphemers, disobedient to parents, unthankful, unholy, without natural affection, trucebreakers, false accusers, incontinent, fierce, despisers of those that are good, traitors, heady, highminded, lovers of pleasures more than lovers of God; having a form of godliness, but denying the power thereof: from such turn away* (2 Timothy 3:1-5).

There is a push from within the Church to be seeker-friendly and move away from all that is supernatural to avoid offending people. I believe that in the quest to reach the world, the Church is alienating God. We now have a seeker-friendly gospel that is no gospel at all. Just as the world is blighted by political correctness, the Church is following suit with spiritual correctness. In today's modern seeker-friendly churches, sin cannot be mentioned, the blood songs cannot be sung, as they are too vile, and the moving of the Holy Spirit is a definite no-no, as that is considered by some as pandemic, ignorant emotionalism. Modernists have the idea that being seeker-friendly with no supernatural power is more palatable to reach the bigger mass. Nothing could be further from the truth. A simple study of the New Testament will reveal that the Holy Spirit's anointing has always been the magnet that draws masses of people to God and salvation conversions. Here are a few verses that epitomize this conclusion:

> *And Jesus returned in the power of the Spirit into Galilee: and there went out a fame of Him through all the region round about* (Luke 4:14).

> *And in the synagogue there was a man, which had a spirit of an unclean devil, and cried out with a loud voice, Saying, Let us alone; what have we to do with thee, thou Jesus of Nazareth? art thou come to destroy us? I know thee who thou art; the Holy One of God. And Jesus rebuked him,*

saying, Hold thy peace, and come out of him. And when the devil had thrown him in the midst, he came out of him, and hurt him not. And they were all amazed, and spake among themselves, saying, What a word is this! for with authority and power He commandeth the unclean spirits, and they come out. And the fame of Him went out into every place of the country round about (Luke 4:33-37).

And when it was day, He departed and went into a desert place: and the people sought Him, and came unto Him, and stayed him, that He should not depart from them (Luke 4:42).

But so much the more went there a fame abroad of Him: and great multitudes came together to hear, and to be healed by Him of their infirmities (Luke 5:15).

And He went forth again by the sea side; and all the multitude resorted unto Him, and He taught them (Mark 2:13).

Tongues makes you more God-sensitive and God-friendly than seeker-friendly.

ENDNOTES

1. Strong's Concordance #G4570.

2. Strong's Concordance #G2842.

3. Strong's Concordance #G3875.

Chapter 7

THE BAPTISM OF THE HOLY GHOST...IT'S EASIER THAN YOU THINK

Having grown in the Pentecostal and Charismatic circle, I've noticed that one of the greatest frustrations for people praying to receive this great gift is, *How do we enter into this great phenomenon?* The frustration is on both parties, the one praying for the person to receive the prayer language and the one waiting to pray in tongues. So many just stand there with their mouths opened thinking somehow that God will come down and wiggle their tongues. Some people are waiting for God to zap them and make them speak in tongues. Let me ask you a question: *Who first began speaking with other tongues?*

Dr. Luke tells Theophilus in his second treatise of the 120 in the Upper Room, "They were filled with the Holy Ghost and began to speak in other tongues" (see Acts 2:4). Was it the Holy Ghost who spoke in tongues or the disciples? Well, it was not the Holy Spirit who spoke but the disciples who began to speak. This simple and yet powerful truth escapes people and is overlooked by those who have read this verse.

People are under the notion that it is the Holy Spirit who forces people to speak. The Holy Ghost is a Gentleman, and He never forces you or anyone to speak with tongues. According to the Word of God, the disciples spoke in tongues as the Holy Spirit gave them the utterance. They opened their mouths by faith and uttered these words which were unknown to them. Look at Paul's words: "For if I pray in an unknown tongue, my spirit prayeth, but my understanding is unfruitful. What is it then? *I will pray with the spirit*, and I will pray with the understanding also" (1 Cor. 14:14-15). Some people have the idea that they can only pray in tongues if they feel inspired. Paul said, "I will pray with the spirit." Praying in tongues is a function of the will.

So how does this apply to us? Exactly the same way! It means until you decide to open your mouth and speak in tongues, nothing is going to happen! Therefore, faith is required! You have to believe that when you open your mouth and speak, the very next words out of your mouth are going to be supplied by the Holy Spirit! This is the part where He gives you the utterance or supplies you with the words. *"As the Spirit gives utterance"* simply means enabled by the already-indwelt Spirit! But you do the speaking! You open your mouth and articulate the expressions that your spirit desires to unleash. It will be your tongue and your vocal cords that actively form words and sounds; however, the Spirit works through the sounds and words unknown to you. Your mind may say to you that this is gibberish. All of us went through this same experience. It is the simple act of opening your mouth in faith and beginning to speak that releases the power of the Holy Ghost to supply the words. This is where you begin to partner with the Holy Spirit! He is not going to give you something that is detrimental to your life.

DO I NEED SOMEONE TO LAY HANDS ON ME BEFORE I RECEIVE THIS GIFT?

Not necessarily! On the day of Pentecost no one laid hands on any of the 120 disciples, yet they all spoke in tongues. In other places in the Book of Acts, while Peter was preaching, it says, "...the Holy Ghost fell on all them which heard the word. And they of the circumcision which believed were astonished, as many as came with Peter, because that on the Gentiles also was poured out **the gift of the Holy Ghost.**

For they heard them speak with tongues, and magnify God" (see Acts 10:44-46). In another place, when Peter and John laid hands on the believers, they received the gift of the Holy Ghost.

> *Now when the apostles which were at Jerusalem heard that Samaria had received the word of God, they sent unto them Peter and John: Who, when they were come down, prayed for them, that they might receive the Holy Ghost: For as yet he was fallen upon none of them: only they were baptized in the name of the Lord Jesus.) Then laid they their hands on them, and they received the Holy Ghost. And when Simon saw that **through laying on of the apostles' hands the Holy Ghost was given...** (Acts 8:14-18).

So while it is good if someone is there to lay hands on you and pray to receive this gift, yet it is not necessary. The Holy Ghost in you can baptize you Himself.

DO I HAVE TO TARRY?

No you do not! Yes, I am aware that Jesus told the disciples to tarry. "And, behold, I send the promise of My Father upon you: but tarry ye in the city of Jerusalem, until ye be endued with power from on high" (Luke 24:49). But that was for the day of Pentecost. We are now living in the reality and fulfillment of Pentecost and the Holy Spirit is here. If we were to take seriously those who believe in the tarrying doctrine, then we would have to go to Jerusalem. Well, that's nonsense. He wants to fill and baptize you now!

WHAT IS THE CRITERIA FOR THIS GIFT?

1. You must be saved.

   Salvation precedes the baptism in the Holy Ghost and not the other way around. Salvation is God's greatest gift to the world, but the baptism of the Holy Ghost is God's greatest gift to His Church.

2. Be open, know and believe that tongues are for you today. If there's an element of doubt, wavering, or doublemindedness, you will short circuit the blessing of God.

3. Be ready to receive and enjoy the gift of tongues.

   Expect the already indwelling Holy Spirit to now come upon you and give you supernatural words unknown to your mind. These unknown words are already within you, they just need to come to your lips and be expressed. I will lead you in prayer, and after repeating the prayer in English, by faith start moving your mouth, form the sounds and give expressions to what is in your spirit. Even though they sound like gibberish, do it, trusting Him to give you the next words. This is the beginning of your partnership with the Holy Spirit. You have to continually choose to yield control of the tongue to your spirit and trust the Holy Spirit to provide the words. Now after prayer, don't just say, "Hallelujah, Hallelujah!" That is known tongue, but you want to speak in tongues.

4. Let's pray, and after prayer let the words that proceed out of your mouth be unknown tongues.

Heavenly Father, thank You for the Holy Spirit who already indwells me. Thank You that it is Your good pleasure to baptize me with the gift of tongues. By faith and in the name of Jesus, I receive the wonderful gift of praying in tongues. And now mighty Holy Spirit, rise up within me, come upon me, and endue me with fresh fire and power. By faith, I now open my mouth and receive your great gift. I will open up my mouth and give expressions to unknown tongues, in the name of Christ Jesus my Lord, Amen!

Now speak and hear the Holy Spirit speaking through you.

Conclusion

101 NUGGETS OF TRUTH

Though satan would love to exalt his demonic doctrine of cessationism over the power of tongues and the indwelling of the Holy Spirit, the Word of God remains clear: Speaking in tongues is the believer's secret gateway to God. Throughout the preceding chapters, many erroneous doctrines have been unveiled to reveal the devil's demonic coup d'etat against the Church. Following are 101 Nuggets of Truth to serve as reminders to the believer of the power and great gift of tongues. You can print these 101 nuggets and take them with you or put them in your Bible in order to be conscious of why you should be praying in tongues.

1. Tongues is the entrance into the supernatural.

2. Tongues is the prayer in the New Testament.

3. Tongues is a direct line to talking to God.

4. Tongues is the believer's direct access to the throne room.

5. Tongues is speaking divine mysteries—divine coded secrets.

6. Tongues is drawing secrets to life's complicated issues.

7. Tongues is prophesying your God-ordained future.

8. Tongues is praying out God's plan for your life.

9. Tongues is knowledge, counsel, and secrets withheld from the wicked.

10. Tongues is the entrance into the realm of the spirit—the miraculous zone.

11. Tongues is strengthening your inner man with might.

12. Tongues keeps you spiritually fit.

13. Tongues is praying things that have been concealed to be revealed.

14. Tongues is decreeing the rhemas of God.

15. Tongues pulls you from the past into the future.

16. Tongues is home improvement and a source of spiritual edification.

17. Tongues is building a strong premise to carry the anointing.

18. Tongues builds and stimulates your faith.

19. Tongues gives you unstoppable progress that your enemies cannot deny.

20. Tongues is giving praise and thanksgiving well unto God.

21. Tongues lines you up with the divine will of God.

22. Tongues is speaking the language and will of God.

23. Tongues is help with your ultimate weakness.

24. Tongues is the ultimate assistance in prayer.

25. Tongues qualifies all things to work for your good.

26. Tongues renders you to be God-inside minded.

27. Tongues makes you miracle-minded.

28. Tongues magnifies God.

29. Tongues enlarges your perspective of God's potency in your life.

30. Tongues gives spiritual refreshing and rest.

31. Tongues hones your sharpness and accuracy in the anointing.

32. Tongues facilitates the entrance into the gifts of the Spirit.

33. Tongues equips you for the wonders of God.

34. Tongues is fine-tuning and sensitizing your spirit man to the voice of God.

35. Tongues is assistance to bring your natural tongue under subjection.

36. Tongues develops intimacy with the Holy Ghost.

37. Tongues is your private conversation with God.

38. Tongues is deep calling unto deep.

39. Tongues accesses revelation knowledge.

40. Tongues taps into the mind of God.

41. Tongues opens the Scriptures to you from a divine perspective rather than an intellectual standpoint.

42. Tongues is part of the armor of God, the lance that will shoot down the enemy.

43. Tongues is the pilum to cause great damage to the kingdom of darkness.

44. Tongues helps you to develop your prayer life.

45. Tongues synchronizes you with the timing of God.

46. Tongues is alignment with the assignment of God.

47. Tongues is a door of utterance and boldness.

48. Tongues is the Holy Spirit searching your heart and praying through you the perfect will of God.

49. Tongues is pulling treasure out of you.

50. Tongues is leaning upon God.

51. Tongues is blowing the ram's horn for battle.

52. Tongues is the rallying sound of victory.

53. Tongues is releasing angels on heavenly assignments to change earthly situations.

54. Tongues is brainstorming session with God.

55. Tongues taps into the creativity of Elohim.

56. Tongues overrules and overturns death assignments against your life.

57. Tongues reverses demonic assignments against your well-being.

58. Tongues removes you from the limitations of the flesh to God's abundant supply of the Spirit.

59. Tongues is making demands upon the power of God.

60. Tongues enables a closer walk with God.

61. Tongues is speaking the hidden wisdom of God.

62. Tongues is the beginning of being led by the Holy Spirit.

63. Tongues is living supernaturally in a natural world.

64. Tongues opens the heavens and charges the atmosphere.

65. Tongues is the release of the shekinah glory.

66. Tongues is getting drunk on the new wine of the Holy Ghost.

67. Tongues is pouring in the oil and wine of the Holy Ghost.

68. Tongues are life-filled words, faith-filled words and anointing-filled words.

69. Tongues lights the fire of God in your life.

70. Tongues delivers you from the scourge of the tongue.

71. Tongues is unlocking every closed prison door in your life.

72. Tongues is a well springing up into the Zoe-God kind of life.

73. Tongues is the beginning and the maintaining of partnership with the Holy Spirit.

74. Tongues is Koinonia with the Parakletos.

75. Tongues is releasing the winds of God to blow in your life.

76. Tongues is the wind in your sail.

77. Tongues is the wind beneath your wings.

78. Tongues unleashes the winds of revival and refreshing in your life.

79. Tongues is refilling empty vessels.

80. Tongues is spirit-to-Spirit communication.

81. Tongues helps in living effectively in the last days.

82. Tongues is the ignition key to walking in the power of God.

83. Tongues is being endued with power from on high.

84. Tongues is rivers of living waters flowing out of you.

85. Tongues is drinking from the river and reservoir of God.

86. Tongues is serving God from your spirit.

87. Tongues enables you to perform your priestly duties.

88. Tongues is building your image of God in you and confidence.

89. Tongues is expressing, enforcing, and declaring the will of God in your life and the earth.

90. Tongues is extracting answers from the indwelling Spirit to solve life's problems.

91. Tongues is praying from your spirit.

92. Tongues is giving your spirit ascendency and power over your flesh.

93. Tongues aids you to mortify the deeds and evil cravings of the flesh.

94. Tongues connects the intercession of the Holy Spirit with your great High Priest Jesus.

95. Tongues is the highest form of the prayer of agreement.

96. Tongues is the divine agreement of the prayers of our earthly and heavenly intercessor with the plans of God.

97. Tongues is the threefold cord that will not be broken.

98. Tongues is ministering to yourself, to the Lord, and unto others.

99. Tongues is worshiping the Father in spirit and in truth.

100. Tongues charges your spiritual battery.

101. Tongues makes you God-friendly rather than seeker-friendly, confuses the devil, and ignites revival.

I count it a great privilege that I am filled with the Holy Ghost with the evidence of speaking in other tongues. There are many things that I value in life, one being my family; but the two greatest things that I value most are my salvation and my prayer language. I can also say with the apostle Paul, "I thank my God, I speak with tongues more than ye all" (1 Cor. 14:18).

As we come to the closing of this book, allow me to echo once again the words of the great apostle Paul, written to the believers in Corinth: "Wherefore, brethren, covet to prophesy, and forbid not to speak with tongues. Let all things be done decently and in order" (1 Cor. 14:39-40).

CONTACT THE AUTHOR

Glenn Arekion Ministries

PO Box 72672
Louisville, KY 40272
USA

mail@glennarekion.org
www.glennarekion.org

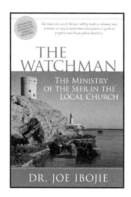

Additional copies of this book and other book
titles from DESTINY IMAGE™ EUROPE
are available at your local bookstore.

We are adding new titles every month!

To view our complete catalog online, visit us at:
www.eurodestinyimage.com

Send a request for a catalog to:

Via Acquacorrente, 6
65123 - Pescara - ITALY
Tel. +39 085 4716623 - Fax +39 085 9431270

"Changing the world, one book at a time."

Are you an author?

Do you have a "today" God-given message?

CONTACT US

We will be happy to review your manuscript
for the possibility of publication:

publisher@eurodestinyimage.com
http://www.eurodestinyimage.com/pages/AuthorsAppForm.htm